SOLID STEPS THROUGH SHIFTING SAND

To Aso,

Thank you for your services on behalf of others. I hope you find in these stories meaningful messages.

All my best,

Mike Carden

SOLID STEPS THROUGH SHIFTING SAND

SHORT STORIES ON A LONG AND GUIDED TRAIL OF TESTS AND WONDERS

HORST WILFRIED RAUHUT
AND
MICHAEL WINFRED RAUHUT

Deeds Publishing | Athens

Published by Deeds Publishing in Athens, GA
www.deedspublishing.com

Printed in The United States of America

Cover design by Mark Babcock
Text layout by Matt King

ISBN 978-1-947309-76-0

Books are available in quantity for promotional or premium use. For information, email info@deedspublishing.com.

First Edition, 2019

10 9 8 7 6 5 4 3 2 1

DEDICATION

To my children,
Birgit with David,
Monika with Kenneth,
and Michael with Sandra,
Favorites among my best Friends[1]

and

To the Soldiers and leaders of the United States Army[2] who selflessly
served—then, as now—so that others might live free.

---

1. 1996
2. In particular, those from the 80th and 83rd Infantry Divisions who, in April 1945, liberated the German towns of Glauchau, Saxony and Halberstadt, Saxony-Anhalt, respectively. Specifically, the thirty-eight 319th Infantry Combat Team Soldiers, predominantly of the 2nd Battalion, who shed their blood liberating Glauchau, April 14-15 (7 of whom were killed; 26 of whom were wounded; 4 additional who died of their wounds; and PFC George Pfeiffer of the Regimental Anti-tank Company who remains missing in action); and the thirteen 329th Infantry Combat Team Soldiers who shed their blood liberating Halberstadt, 11 April (2 of whom were killed and 11 of whom were wounded in action). Throughout my service my father asked me to convey his personal and familial thanks to fellow Soldiers and service-members which I have done dutifully to this day. See Honor Rolls in Appendices.

IN HONOR OF

Magdalena and Horst Rauhut

"Whoever pursues righteousness and kindness will find life, righteousness, and honor."

— Proverbs 21:21

IN MEMORY OF

Birgit Wingard [Rauhut]
June 12, 1959 to April 20, 2019

Beloved Daughter, Sister, Aunt, Wife, Mentor, and Friend
who was called home after her courageous battle.
Birgit's creativity and kindness, authenticity and sincerity, courage
and compassion, and faith illuminate our path.

*"But the path of the righteous is like the light of dawn, which shines
brighter and brighter until full day."*

—Proverbs 4:18

CONTENTS

FOREWORD

Solid Steps through Shifting Sand is an inspiring reminder of life's unforeseen circumstances and the importance of relationships in forging our major decisions. While a story about generations of a German and German-American family, it is deeper than that. It captures a vivid portrait of faith, family, and selfless service.

I first became acquainted with Horst Rauhut's son Mike in 2002 when I returned from Afghanistan and was stationed at Ft. Hood, Texas. We met at an Officer Christian Fellowship bible study. I knew he was serving as the operations officer for the battalion that I was slated to command and hoped that he would still be there when I took the colors. By the time I took command of the 1st Battalion, 22nd Infantry Regiment, we had deployed to Iraq in the first year of the war. I was grateful that not only did I have the privilege to serve with an outstanding operations officer who later became my executive officer, but I also had someone to confide my deepest thoughts with about my faith as we both endured daily fighting as infantrymen during the hunt and capture of Saddam Hussein. We have remained close friends ever since.

As you read these pages, you are struck with a sense of how faith in Christ leads us through the darkest times of political turmoil, threat of war, suffering, deprivation, loss of family members in battle or to collateral damage, and then find a vision for the future amidst the hunger and ashes of the aftermath. As tragic as those scenarios seem, Horst Rauhut never wavered to see the beauty, the possibility of hope, and better still, to act on those glimmers to see God's plan unfold to better life and understanding.

I hope you will be as enriched as I was when reading these fascinating vignettes about how a normal, hard-working family triumphed through generational faith that continues to this day. It comes as no surprise after seeing Horst's son Mike in action on both spiritual and actual battlefields.

— Steve Russell
LTC, US Army (Ret)
Former Member US Congress
Author of *"We Got Him!"—A Memoir of the Hunt and Capture of*
Saddam Hussein

1. INTRODUCTION

"As for man, his days are like grass; he flourishes like a flower of the field; the wind blows over it, and it is gone, and its place remembers it no more."

—*Psalm 103: 15-16*

Horst Wilfried Rauhut flourished for eighty-one eventful years. Although he is gone and the psalmist's epitaph rings true, his story and our memories survive. Dad ultimately departed this life thankful and joyful. To the end immensely loving and practical, he instructed whom to thank, how to order his affairs (which he, of course, had already ordered), and how to care for family and friends. He took Moses[3] and Matthias Claudius to heart when it came to life and longevity. Dad passed away in the early morning hours of November 2, 2011.

"Wilfried," Dad's middle name, means "desiring peace." One imagines how prescient Dad's father was in May 1930, perhaps influenced by his own experience as a soldier of the Great War and the turmoil that ensued in Germany following World War One. Dad's temperament bore his middle name true. As you read, you will feel Dad's desire for personal, familial, and broader peace. Dad was a realist, however, having experienced war's horror as a child. He helped his blind mother and two

---

3. Psalm 90

1

older sisters survive in post-WWII Germany, sensed acutely the looming threat of communism and war from the Soviet Union, and escaped with his own family to the United States. Perhaps for some of these reasons he felt compelled to pass along the middle name "Winfred"—"maker of peace"—seeking closure.

Nearing Dad's retirement, we encouraged him to capture our family story. My sisters and I would neither recall all the rich details, nor capture Dad's humor without his written word. As we read these pages of our parent's life experiences, our own memories flush with emotion. We hear our mother's thankful spirit as she describes our humble, unique heritage, reminding us to love and stay grounded. We hear our Dad's German accent, considered delivery with timed, dramatic pauses, and his infectious laugh. His authenticity cascades forth and causes us to smile or cry, if for no other reason than our father's joy in telling a story or joke, sharing a memory, and conveying life's meaning.

Many of us are blessed to know and share life's journey with people we love and from whom we draw inspiration and strength. Our Dad was one of those people. Through difficult times, Dad's character took shape and manifested in beautiful ways to our benefit. Having had the personal honor to know and grow close to incredibly gifted, loving, and genuine men and women of character and virtue, I am struck by my Dad's humble immensity; his quiet certitude; his genuine love for others. He, of course, would be first to point out that his strength was not his own and derived from the One who gives and takes away.

We hope you will enjoy his immigrant story, told in his familiar and personal manner. We trust you will connect with our Dad, Horst Rauhut, and our Mom, Magdalena [Winkel], from whom we continue to learn and for whom we remain eternally thankful. For those of you who have met us, we hope too that in meaningful ways we reflect some of their light. Finally, we encourage you to share your own stories to edify and demonstrate love for others.

"So teach us to number our days, that we may get a heart of wisdom."

—*Psalm 90:12*

NATURAL MAN

Conceived and nourished
by a woman
in a wonderful way,
he comes to see
the light of day,
to hear,
and does not
recognize deceit.
He lusts, desires,
and sheds his tear,
despises and honors,
experiences joy
and danger,
believes and doubts,
imagines and teaches,
accepts as true
nothing and everything,
builds up and destroys,
sleeps and wakes up,
grows, wastes away,
and wears his hair
brown and grey.
All this lasts
about eighty years.
Then he gathers
to his fathers,
never to return.

Matthias Claudius, 1740—1815

2. BACKGROUND ECHOES
1890 – 1945

SHORT STORIES OF EVENTS
ON FOUR CONTINENTS,

BEGINNING IN THE LATE 1800'S,

WHICH INFLUENCED OUR LIVES,

OUR FUTURE, AND ORIENTATION.

THE SERVANT OF THE SICK

"Greater love has no one than this, that he lay down his life for his friends."

—John 15:13

A friend may be a stranger. As a boy, he heard the good news, which warmed his heart. As a young man, he heard the call to a foreign mission field and followed it like others in his family. Subsequently, he was trained and met the lady of his life. Together they shipped out to India, several weeks at sea, many months on land. Beautiful Bangalore in southern India was their destination. Highly situated, about 3000 feet above sea level, the city offered a good climate. It was also the seat of the British governor and of the military in the south. There he spread and lived the good news among the Indian people.

True missionaries are not just talkers, but doers. In fact, the way we understand their tasks, missionaries must be able to work in practical ways. There is a time for everything, a time to love, a time to establish a family. Bangalore was the location for that, too. There is also a time for death, even multiple deaths, and it raged through southern India. Cholera is caused by vibrio cholera, a germ with a little paddle, which leads to vigorous self-motion in fluids. It flourishes in contaminated water. Within the intestines it dehydrates and poisons the body. We do not know how many patients he cared for, how many hundreds died, how many survived the epidemic. Had they only been given clean water to drink! Now there is so much more known about fighting the dreaded disease, so its occurrence is more limited than in the 1800s. At the end of his strength, our missionary fell prey to cholera, too, and died. To the sick and dying, the friendly servant was no longer a stranger. Mercy spared him from the horrors of the twentieth century.

Left behind were his young widow [Ida Winkel (geb. Herre)] and his only son [Ernst Winkel; "Erny"], born after his death. But everything turned out well since he had a covenant with the Employer he served. He also had an agreement with a European friend to care for his family if anything should happen to him. Thus, the missionary's son Erny—your grandfather [Magdalena's Dad]—as a teen-ager came to Russia, to his "uncle" in St. Petersburg. In due time, the attractive young widow remarried [Metzker] and had three more sons. Marty [Martin] became a noted painter of Indonesian and German landscapes [We have many of his sketches and paintings in our homes]. Fred [Sigi] trapped and fished in northern Manitoba, Canada. Rudy [Rudolf] was put onto a prison ship [Prisoner of War] in Indonesia during World War II, then died in the Pacific Ocean after a torpedo attack. His wooden sea chest survived. But these are separate stories, with far-reaching connections around the world.

EARLY VISION WARNS

"The vision concerns a time yet to come."

— *Daniel 10:14b*

Ernst had lost his father before he was born. As a young boy, he came to his "uncle' in St. Petersburg, as I related in the preceding story.[4] In 1905, when Ernst was fourteen, the Russian-Japanese war broke out. His German "uncle" worked for the Russian Foreign Office. From the Siberian front, ciphered messages arrived. His "uncle" had big codebooks at home, and there he deciphered the messages while Ernst did his homework for school. Since then the world has come a long way in the area of state security and got it out of the living room. So, I believe, this story is without parallel. Unusual is also that I can pass it on, about one century later, due to our family relationship.

But the story becomes even more unusual. Ernst attended a college in Germany that prepared its students for colonial farming. A real uncle in Germany paid for it. This was still the colonial era before the First World War when Germany had colonies too. Subsequently, Ernst was sent to Cameroon in western Africa as a plantation manager. When World War

---

4. Cousin Sylvia Winkel (eldest daughter of Mom's brother Gerhard and Tante Esther) shared the included photo (p118) and wrote, "…taken in St. Petersburg where Grandpa was educated in a wealthy family. I remember that he often told us about the extra-large Christmas Tree in "his family", wholly decorated with red and polished apples."

One broke out, the British took him as prisoner to the Isle of Wight in the English Channel. The Dutch neutrality was honored at that time. Thus, the British and the Germans exchanged prisoners in the Netherlands. Ernst had to stay there for the rest of the war. In church Ernst met the Blok family and their beautiful daughter who operated a "winkel" or little store. Ironically, that was his last name, meaning angle in German. When the war ended in 1918, the Germans lost their colonies. Good riddance; at least in this area they were ahead of France and Britain. Ernst, now a plantation manager for the Dutch on Sumatra, never forgot the little Dutch girl from the 'winkel." But when his mother wrote that Elizabeth Maria had married, he tried to get her off his mind until a Dutch acquaintance arrived in the colonies.[5] Asked how many children Maria had, the man answered that she was still unmarried. At that time existed still a certain civil order of events prior to having children. Ernst immediately sent a telegram to his Maria who accepted, was betrothed in her homeland with a white glove, and then sailed to Sumatra. This formality [white glove marriage] was customary to protect an engaged lady during a long sea voyage.

The misunderstanding was explained by Ernst's wife, Maria Elizabeth. It was her sister, Elizabeth Maria, who had previously married. Thereafter followed a time of seclusion at the edge of a colonial jungle. The happy couple lived on Java and on Sumatra and their three children [Ernst Jr., Gerhard, and Magdalena] were born on these Indonesian islands while Ernst managed plantations growing rubber and other tropical crops. During this time in Indonesia, Maria had a strange vision. She saw a European city with four arches and her husband Ernst running out of one of these arches. Such a place she had never seen before.

In 1929, the world economic crisis had begun, and in the mid-thirties, after many years in the tropics, the family went on a European furlough by ocean liner. They stayed in Germany and in the Netherlands,

---

5. Dad shared with me that Ernst's mother was not keen on her son's relationship and so played on the confusion of Maria's name as both a family first and middle name.

where they received the disconcerting news that Ernst's high-paying job had been eliminated. From his severance pay he bought a small farm in Grüenhof, Pomerania near the Polish border [Mom, Uncle Gerhard, and I visited Grüenhof in October 1990 when I was serving in the Berlin Brigade]. Sandy soil and poor yields soon caused economic hardship. To make matters complicated, German law at the time made it difficult to sell the farm again. But eventually it did sell, although with financial loss. With his multiple language skills, including German, Russian, Dutch, English, Malaysian, and others, Ernst would have been a natural choice for radio employment. However, his Christian and non-political conviction made him unacceptable for this kind of prestigious job. In the Rhineland, he ended up taking care of pigs fed with kitchen waste. Within a few years, he had gone from feast to famine and worked in a humiliating situation.

Soon the Second World War broke out. To help after devastating air raids on the cities, Ernst was drafted into an air raid assistance organization at home, to which Russian prisoners of war were later assigned. Slowly but surely, this unnecessary war came to its gory conclusion. In 1945, the western allies steadily advanced, and the prisoners had to be escorted east, for which task Ernst with his Russian language skill was selected. However, the prisoners were quite apprehensive about meeting their Soviet communist "liberators." So, one after another disappeared on this trek, until Ernst was the only person remaining. He promptly went to Glauchau, Saxony where his wife and daughter had gone to stay with relatives after their evacuation from the heavily bombarded Rhineland.

When American troops arrived and occupied[6] the city, they went

---

6. See "Narrative Account of Action, 14 April 1945". 2nd Battalion, 319th Infantry Regiment, 80th Infantry Division fought for and cleared the town by 2400. "Glauchau, Germany. Arrived on 14 April 1945 at 1600. Departed on 16 April 1945 at 1300." http://www.80thdivision.com/UnitHistories/319thInfReg_UnitHistory_APR45-partial_1.pdf (accessed March 18, 2018).

from house to house. Adult males were usually taken prisoners, since they could be soldiers. But Ernst was let go when his American captor found a New Testament in his pocket [Mom shared with me that the U.S. soldier said his own mother told him to read his Bible every day while deployed].[7]

Now we have to enter the Allies' Treaty of Yalta, which laid down

---

7. Some of my Mom's fondest childhood memories were made when staying with the Meyner family in Glauchau. Mom's Uncle Meyner rented the large home for his family practice (see photo p119). Mom recalled many joyful memories from her time in Glauchau, affirmed by my Tante Irmgard Meyner, mom's cousin and a daughter of Dr. Meyner. By April 1945, Grandpa Winkel reunited with his wife, children, and the Meyner family in Glauchau. About 30 German refugees—all women and children displaced from the east—had joined them and lived on the first floor of the residence. Mom described hearing explosions and gun fire from the fighting above while all huddled in the basement below. When the U.S. soldiers cleared their area and home, the soldiers told the family they could not stay. The soldiers directed them to go to the kasserne for food and shelter. Despite the directive, Grandpa Winkel humbly asked for food for the family and refugees. Only there for a few days and not permitted to give away food, the soldiers exercised compassionate discretion, giving the women and children staple and telling Grandpa to check certain locations around the property after the unit left. Grandpa found beans, coffee, and sugar in abundance. The Russians arrived shortly after the U.S. departure and required Grandpa Winkel to report to them the following day. Grandpa Winkel fled that night based on the vision and his wife's admonition. On bible account: Grandpa carried his small bible in his breast pocket. Upon searching Grandpa the soldier asked him what it was. Grandpa Winkel said it was his bible, whereupon the soldier commented on his mother's guidance. Grandpa said it was a good book and encouraged the soldier to heed his mom's advice and read it.

U.S. Army account: http://www.80thdivision.com/80th-OperationalHistory/80thOperHist-Apr45_Pt1.pdf (accessed 18 March 2018). From "History, 80th Infantry Division, April 1945". The operational history of the 80th Infantry Division, 14 April 1945: "The 2d Bn 319th Infantry also experienced great difficulty in performing it's mission of taking GLAUCHAU (K-3958). It moved from the assembly area at 0740. Considerable small arms, automatic weapons, bazooka, mortar and sniper fire was encountered. A particularly strong defensive position located in the center of town was knocked out only with the greatest difficulty. Elements of the 702d Tank Bn and the 811th Tank Destroyer Bn (SP) in support, fired at buildings at point blank range to successfully knock out enemy strong points. By nightfall, the 2d Bn had cleared all but the southeast section of town where groups of fanatical Nazis fought."

how post-war Germany should be carved up into occupation zones. Thereby many areas in Germany which were conquered by American troops ended up in the Soviet occupation zone. In due time, it became a dreaded communist dictatorship that invented the Iron Curtain and the Berlin Wall.

When the Soviets got into Glauchau and heard that Ernst spoke Russian, they wanted him to work for them. At that time, Maria remembered her vision in Indonesia more than a decade earlier. She recognized that Glauchau was the European city of her vision. While it would have been natural for Ernst to stay with his family and provide for them as a farm worker when food was scarce, it became clear that he must leave or risk his safety and life. He took the early warning and promptly fled through the arch shown in Maria's vision. This had far-reaching consequences for our family, for later we met in the Rhineland and I married his wonderful daughter, who accompanied me on our immigration to America.

THE THANKFUL SOWER

*"As the rain and the snow come down from heaven, and do not return
to it without watering the earth and making it bud and flourish, so
that it yields seed for the sower and bread for the eater, so is My word
that goes out from My mouth: It will not return to Me empty, but will
accomplish what I desire and achieve the purpose for which I sent it."*

—Isaiah 55: 10-11

My mother's father [Thomas Klose, 1852-1935] belonged to a successful family of merchants who dealt in butter and related products and
sold them by horse-drawn wagon. On one trip home through a large
forested area, a thief and murderer joined my Grandpa Klose's father
[name unknown], then killed him with a knife and stole his leather
pouch containing the day's income. Evidently such crime so common
by gun today was committed by knife in the previous century, however
rarely. The horses knew their way home by heart and sadly delivered a
dead coachman. I do not know whether the evildoer was apprehend-
ed or not. Enough money remained in this family for my Grandfather
Klose and his brothers to learn a trade, an uncommon privilege in those
days. Thus, grandfather became a tailor. Perhaps through his trade, he
made the friendship of the widowed administrator of a large farm estate
and married his daughter [Marianne Goral]. The grandparents [Thomas
Klose and Marianne Goral] bought a small farm. Since my Grandpa

was little and not very strong, he relied on his energetic wife for much of the physical work on the farm. Hard work was a woman's chore anyway, besides bearing and raising many children. These grandparents were unique, as I will show below, and I wish I could have met them. But we lived far apart, and soon they died.

Besides rain or snow showers, much needed on the sandy farm, they received in church recurring showers of the good news for their souls. Grandma's faith was mostly expressed by her attitude in the village where she helped neighbors in medical need with her thorough knowledge of herbal and other natural treatments. She [Marianne Goral] was a person of deeds rather than words, and applied remedies, even discipline, effectively and efficiently. It had to be that way considering the abundance of her chores. Among her children, there was one boy more prone to get into mischief than all the others, an imaginative lad who later became a successful small businessman. Of the local opportunities for trouble, he identified and explored many (such as letting their neighbor's pigs escape from the pen so that they could roam in gardens and fields). His misdeeds did not endear him to his mom. So, one night she decided to deliver his well-deserved punishment. The era preceded by decades the arrival of electricity or other forms of affluence, e.g., each family member having an own bed. Thus, grandpa shared his bed with his naughty boy. So, there she came with a leather belt into the dark bedroom, lifted the fluffy feather bed cover, and wholeheartedly thrashed the body below her. Grandpa [Thomas Klose] was in deep sleep, but woke up quickly and cried, "Wife, what are you doing?!" However, it was too late. He had already taken his spanking, while their son had had the foresight of sleeping in the hayloft.

There has been much debate about corporal punishment resulting in its banishment for psychological reasons. Ever since, disrespect for order and authority, even teenage crime, have increased. Now we have two positions on this subject. One states that such punishment irreversibly mars personalities, even leads to lack of compassion. The other one claims it is good for the soul.[8] I can only reiterate that Grandpa's spanking did not adversely affect his compassion, and I know this straight from my mother. Here is the story.

With their many children, the grandparents could not make ends meet on the farm. So, they rented it, took their children to the Bremen area, and worked in a factory. They took all the children but one, my mother [Johanna Klose] as a little girl. The intent was to pick her up at a later time. Meanwhile, she stayed with the family who leased the farm, and Grandpa sent money there for clothing and shoes. When he later came to visit, he saw the girl with bare feet and asked about the shoes. The man then showed him shoes much too big for a small child, whereupon Grandpa took them and threw them through the room, then took his little girl with him to the rest of the family.

The story about Grandpa [Thomas Klose] that touches me most portrays him as a sower spreading seed by hand onto his field, either wheat or rye. He consistently walked and planted straight from one end to the other; then paused, took his cap from his head, prayed and thanked God. Then he returned straight ahead and parallel; paused again; took the cap from his head; prayed for the needed harvest and thanked God. Thus, he repeated the sowing process until the whole field was filled with blessed seed, this mysterious form of life for future sustenance. How much sense of dependence and humility are expressed in this scene! He anticipated that the good Lord would come through again with a harvest of grain, and plainly thanked him. But you could not do this properly with your cap on your head, this instrument of deceitful know-how. So, he took it off. Well, in Europe people even take their hat off when they greet another person on the street. How much more respect belongs to the Lord of all! Does this attitude also apply to our sophisticated day and age? I believe it does, and I am certain that it works. To quote Matthias Claudius, "We seek many new arts, but deviate farther from the goal." He said

---

8. Despite Dad's posits herein, he was not one to use corporal punishment.

that about two hundred years ago already. What is our true goal anyway in this vastly expanding technological age? To put more high-powered guns on the street, or to continually foul up our environment?[9] Grandpa's simple life was in tune with Claudius' wise and balanced thinking, well into his late years when he sang thoughtful hymns with his clear voice while he guarded his milk cows on the meadow.

---

9. Dad was a man ahead of his time with respect to social and environmental issues.

GOLDEN YEARS END

"Do not say, 'Why were the old days better than these?' For it is not wise to ask such question."

—Ecclesiastes 7:10

From independent sources, including my mother's report, we know that the time before World War I were golden years. Prosperity in Germany began already in the 1870's. There was an unshaken belief in progress and new development. New firms were founded, and anyone with some ability and industry could turn his labor or effort into gold. Of course, society consisted of various classes. But even newlyweds like my parents lived well and beyond their basic needs. Actually, all of central Europe and Britain enjoyed prosperity and order. Eastern Europe with its agricultural basis was another story. Even the eastern provinces of Prussia were economically affected, such that my mother's parents [Thomas Klose and Marianne Goral] could not make ends meet on their small farm. They rented it and moved to the Bremen area in northern Germany where a processing plant for Australian wool provided them with much better means. The westward trek of our family began already then in the 1890's, not with our immigration to America seventy years later.

Politically, Europe was a world of nations for two hundred years: proud, selfish, and independent. Common citizens of any nation desired only happiness, while their noble politicians, pursuing power and prestige, managed to mislead them into the misery of World War I. Nobody wanted it, but everybody followed their flag with naive enthusiasm when a futile exercise of selfish diplomacy failed. Widespread nationalism was the cause of war, not the two shots in Sarajevo that killed the Austrian archduke and his wife. If assassinations would suffice to start a world war, we could have another one every year. On the German side, geographically surrounded by many nations, it took caution and a well-balanced diplomacy to avoid war. Bismarck knew and practiced this. When he was dismissed in 1890, the British published a cartoon showing a pilot leaving the ship. Since then, some of the emperor's imprudent speeches helped destabilize the perceived balance of power, even though there was still no good reason for war. However, pride and evil became an invincible pair that turned over and changed forever the old world of Europe. "Would it not be better for you to be wronged?" Such an unthinkable position would have been better, but I do not know whether it was ever practiced in history.

When the die was cast, my parents [Adolf Gustav Rauhut and Johanna Klose] were left without alternatives. He was drafted, and she was left behind with two children.[10] Before they parted, they acted old-fashioned; they pledged to each other absolute loyalty, and then practiced it for the duration of the war and beyond. Thus, he moved into war, a farmer's boy, then city worker and father. He had been a volunteer with the Prussians earlier in the century and was honorably discharged as a bugle player in 1905.[11]

Now, in 1914, the establishment remembered him as a good man.

---

10. Adolf Gustav Rauhut, Sr. was mobilized into the 64 Reserve-Infantrie-Regiment, 1st Garde Reserve Division and Korps. His father, Andreas Rauhut, had served in the elite Prussian Guards in Berlin. By this time, Johanna had given birth three times – Maria Anna, Elisabeth Hermine, and Klära Rosalie Rauhut. Maria Anna (23 Oct 1908-25 Nov 1979) and Klära Rosalie or "Klaerchen" Rauhut (23 Mar 1912 – 27 Mar 1945) survived. Elisabeth Hermine Rauhut, born the second child, died a month after her 1 September birth in 1910.

11. 1902-1905: Served with the 7. West Prussian Infantrie Regiment, Nr. 155.

His comrades thought he was a good man too. They had to eat and chose him as cook, for all four war years, because he could be trusted with all food resources received and would pass them on.

From everything we know, the First World War terrified participating soldiers on both sides, and I do not understand why it is called the Great War in French and English. Since gross details have been described in multiple languages, there is no need to repeat them here. The result was a widespread conviction that it was the war that ended all wars. How profoundly wicked must human nature be that this wish could not be fulfilled. The emperor was said to have shown a withdrawn expression when he visited the Western front in 1917. There was no sign of conviction in victory, but the war went on for another year.

Even though my dad was serving at a field kitchen, he was not out of harm's way. People in his vicinity were maimed or killed by artillery, but he was spared. When he told stories, I never heard him glorify the war. Instead he reported meeting enemy soldiers in no-man's land to exchange gifts for Christmas, and funny, friendly encounters with civilians. There was the story about his comrades buying onions in a French store, and he gave them the Polish word *cebula*, which caused confusion and laughter. Another time, they fried chicken, but someone had put a glass panel on the chimney, which caused a lot of smoke and choking, but the light kept shining through the chimney. He certainly loved people, and he came home in one piece and with a positive mindset. But that was not universally true. I met someone who lost his mind in battle, someone else who became quite melancholic, and someone who was unusually quiet in later years. He reported that he survived artillery attacks by jumping continually from one fresh crater into the next, a statistically sound practice since a local double hitter would be unlikely. He did not believe that people should undergo such strenuous exercise for hours.

Noteworthy people came home from this war. One was the remarkable Erich Maria Remarque, whose book *All Quiet on the Western Front* I read as a youth. He described Corporal Himmelstoss ("Push to Heaven"), who cynically trained soldiers so that they would not be confused at the Berlin-Lehrte train station where they would have to go down and up from one platform to the next. So, he chased them with his whistle from one side of a large table to the next and made them crawl under it repeatedly. Only once did I hear about a more cynical drill, when soldiers were ordered into their lockers and pulled the doors behind them. On the tone of a whistle they had to open their locker doors, stick out their heads, and cry "Cuckoo." I recall that Remarque was nominated for the Nobel Peace Prize and the Nobel Prize in Literature.

Another corporal returned from war in order to cause the second war. While this man was unteachable, a famous, young naval officer by the name of Martin Niemöller learned, studied theology, and became the corporal's spiritual foe, then landed in a concentration camp from 1937 to 1945 for his conviction. An eighteen-year-old volunteer, soon to become a brave lieutenant, also got onto the corporal's enemy list, the playwright Carl Zuckmayer, whose honest and realistic autobiography is one of the best sources for understanding European and German history of the terrible century's first half. In his "Captain of Köpenick" he lets us witness one of the most hilarious incidents of military Prussia. Zuckmayer, Remarque, Brecht and many other prominent writers had to flee Germany for their lives to America, the haven of liberty. We later immigrants "discovered" in the seventies Zuckmayer's two-hundred-year-old farm in the green mountains near Barnard, Vermont, on the basis of literature hints.[12] There he worked for the survival of his family in the 1940's and wrote the most relevant play for post-war performance, "The Devil's General." While those men escaped with their lives, and Niemöller only did so by miracle, many other excellent people did not survive the corporal's wrath. But I should really tell only one story at a time.

---

12. Dad and I visited this farm on one of our trips.

ONE GUILDER AND THE CUCKOO

"If you believe, you will receive whatever you ask for in prayer".

—Matthew 21:22

Tough times followed the Great War, a fitting disillusion, since no war is great. No identity, no stability, no economy, no work, no money followed the war. Ironically, people had too much money for several years, considering the galloping inflation rate when one loaf of bread cost a few billion marks. As radicals on the left and right fought over turf in the big cities, many civilians died in local urban wars. Germany's first opportunity for democracy was ill received because of hunger and destitution. Although some great democratic personalities appeared on the political scene, the so-called Weimar Republic failed. There were too many parties, too little consensus, too much need, and too much radicalism. The Federal Republic of Germany learned from history and included in its constitution of 1949 a five percent clause, thereby eliminating radical groups (which usually receive only one to three percent of the popular vote but are disproportionately more vocal) from the legislature. All this made the social-political environment of the 1920's suitable for the Christian experience, which my parents were wise to practice. Since then, through the rest of this century, the world has sadly created many similar opportunities elsewhere, which suggests an excellent global market for the Good News.

Dutch Christians invited starving German children to their homes, and my oldest sister [Maria Anna Rauhut] became one of their guests. This became my family's first contact with Holland. Years went on with real economic hardship, and mother would do home-work to pay for basic needs. Tedious night work strained her eyes to such an extent that it later contributed to her blindness. She firmly believed and prayed for solutions in pressing needs. Dad found a good job but needed a bicycle for transportation, when mom's prayer was answered in the form of one Dutch guilder. She reported that the exchange into marks provided the exact amount needed for Dad's bike.

My parents experienced also the opportunity provided by a certain cuckoo, this European bird whose lovely voice we heard in the woods, who earlier had invented the idea of foster parents (by others), and later came to America by the thousands enshrined in cuckoo clocks. However, their cuckoo was stamped on the back of a nice living room cabinet, which they wanted, but normally could not afford. With the cuckoo stamped on its back, it had been taken away from people in deep debt, and was then cheaply sold. The cabinet, joined by a handsome book cabinet with glass and an organ[13], enhanced the comfort of our living room. Good books were a treat for the mind, and music praised His goodness.

---

13. My sister Monika Harris (geb. Rauhut) has the pump organ in her home today.

ON THE WAY TO BIELEFELD

"The eternal God is your refuge, and underneath are the everlasting arms..."

—*Deuteronomy 33:27*

"It is better to take refuge in the Lord than to trust in man."

—*Psalm 118:8*

Everyone is unique, but some people are more unique than others. My father's youngest sister, Erna, belonged to the latter category. She lived to almost ninety-two, sharp and humorous. Blessed with an excellent memory, she shared with me family experiences otherwise unknown to us so that I can pass them on.

She grew up on her parent's farm of 30 morgens[14] [Andreas and Karoline Rauhut (geb. Jaensch)]. Since one morgen includes only 250 square-meters, these people had a very small farm by American standards. She and her next sister Lena liked to do chores with their animals: cows, calves, pigs, geese, and chickens. There was also one horse for plowing and some occasional riding by the children.

---

14. 1 morgen = .62 acres so a 30-morgen farm is about 18.5 acres.

When she [Erna] was ninety-one, I had the opportunity to spend five days with her. Every morning, she fixed breakfast and then told me interesting stories of events that happened between about 1910 and 1945. Thereby, she shed some light into the circumstances of life not mentioned in history books.

"We went three kilometers to school, through wind and weather. In winter we could skate, since the creek through our meadows was frozen. Many shoe soles were worn out, while shoes were scarce particularly during World War I. My childhood and youth were without trouble. However, there were foreboding signs of coming dangers. In 1913, there was a total eclipse of the sun. The teacher said, 'Great changes are going to happen; eventful years are beginning.' How right he was."

"People do not wage wars, governments do. Military mobilization was set for August 1, 1914. Fearful farmers talked about politics that they did not understand. Many tears were flowing when the first war casualties were announced, including some neighbors and my cousins' husbands. Our churches held special services to pray for peace. The war lasted four years and ended with an armistice in November 1918. Emperor Wilhelm II had to step down. Then the church bells rang sadly because our beloved homeland in the east of Germany was turned over to Poland in the context of a lost war. Now we had to decide whether we wanted to stay in Poland or go to Germany. At that time, many youths decided to go there."

"In the nearby village of Morschaler lived the Duchess of Bismarck-Bohlen. She owned a large estate and an orphanage for a hundred children. It was a magnificent sight when she and the children came to church, all the children uniformly dressed and holding hands as they entered the church in groups. In 1923, she and the German children had to leave and they said good-bye to us. The children of Polish descent were taken by the Polish buyer of the orphanage. The duchess and her sister, named Mother Eva, went to the city of Chemnitz. Now the remaining German people felt deserted and grieved over these immigrants. I left then, too, with two other girls. Assisted by "flight helpers" we went illegally across the Polish border. The first train station on the other side was Neumittelwalde. From there I wrote to my brothers in Düsseldorf and Duisburg that I arrived under "German sky," which made them laugh heartily."

Finally, the girls came to Berlin to stay with Erna's sister Ida. At station Alexanderplatz was a stop for the streetcar to Nieder-Schoenhausen, where Ida and her husband lived. "Not quite eighteen and curious about the city, I wanted to see something of Berlin on this cold and rainy day in January of 1921. So, I said to the other girls to step in. It was streetcar number 48." They entered the door by the driver, who looked at them and asked, "Well, young ladies, where are you going?" Always quick with her tongue, she answered "To my sister in Nieder-Schoenhausen!" "Then just turn around," he replied. There she saw her brother-in-law, the driver's friend. They both knew that the girls were coming, but not exactly when and had looked out for them. Such was their friendly welcome in Berlin. On the next day already, one of the girls found a job, and the other one went to relatives near Berlin. Erna herself worked for the next six months in Berlin-Wilmersdorf, and then for two years in Düsseldorf, close to her favorite brother.

"After that time, I became homesick," she continued, "and visited my parents [Andreas Johann Rauhut and Karoline geb. Jaensch] in Poland. They did not want to let me go again. So, I stayed at home for one year, during which time I met my future husband. We got married in 1925. Our permission to stay in Poland ran out in 1926. So, we both went to Düsseldorf, where we raised a family and built a house." There she lived her long life and was blessed with twelve grandchildren, six great-grandchildren, and one great-great-grandchild.

When I look at her life, I see four outstanding traits: wit, an open house for everybody, personal discipline, and faith. It is hard to comprehend how this lady and so many others went through two vicious world wars. During the second war, she visited her sister Lena on the little farm

in the eastern country which was temporarily again in German possession. When the inevitable departure time arrived, Lena used poetic
language to ease the pain:

"If we don't see each other in this Welt, we see each other in Bielefeld."

In her rhyme, Welt is the German word for World. Well, this turned
out to be prophetic, as we will see.

In due course, the terror of war was coming to an end. Soviet forces
pressed hard on Poland and Germany. Grandfather [Andreas Rauhut]
was dead already and buried in Polish soil. But Grandma was alive and
fled west with Lena's family. So, they came to the ruins of Berlin late in
1944, under grim and different circumstances. At that time, this century's flood of multimillion refugees began which by now approaches
half a billion people worldwide. We have to go back to the third century
A.D. to see migration of such scale and proportion to the total world
population.

At the Berlin Zoo train station, Grandmother managed to separate
herself from her daughter's family. She had good intent and just desired
to see her oldest daughter Ida. There is an intersection from where two
main streets go off at an angle, Kurfürstendamm and Kaiserallee, where
Ida lived. Well, Grandma in her eighties took the wrong street and
walked for miles until she was exhausted. A church deaconess observed
and asked her where she belonged, but she could not get a satisfactory
answer. So, Grandma was put into a nursing home in Spandau, completely separated from her family, and her family knew nothing of her.
Meanwhile, the train had to move on, and with it Lena's family. Where
did they stop and eventually put their lives together again? In the city of
Bielefeld (If not in this "Welt," then in Bielefeld).

We are all in transit, but our story has a happy ending. Grandma
could not remember Ida's address in Berlin, but she remembered Erna's

address in Düsseldorf. Ida was then informed, visited, and took care of her mother. After all, we belong to a caring family.

SINGER SAM

"Here we do not have an enduring city, but we are looking for the city that is to come."

—Hebrews 13:14

"As for man, his days are like grass; he flourishes like a flower of the field; the wind blows over it, and it is gone, and its place remembers it no more."

—Psalm 103: 15-16

While your Great Grandfather [Ernst Gottfried Winkel] served the sick in India, Sam served his community and church in the remote hills of eastern America. We do not know where he came from, but it is safe to assume that he was not a new immigrant since these parts were usually settled by secondary immigrants, many people from New England states particularly Massachusetts. Generally early immigration focused on our northeastern states or on Virginia. Virginia's excess flow of people spread mostly into the Southeast, and also to the Midwest, as commemorated by Virginia Road in Crystal Lake, Illinois.

Sam operated a small farm in our vicinity [Haskell Flats, Hinsdale, New York] and provided firewood to the one-room schoolhouse down the road, like other neighbors. He also made some building improvements on the school. It appears that he needed extra money to get by. A new church was being built, a cooperative effort by the Methodists and Baptists of the area, who until that time met in the school or in barns. Eight pioneer families of the valley donated stained-glass windows to the sanctuary. Sam Rude, although qualified, was not among these donors. He was one of the first trustees, accepted the new building on dedication day from a major community supporter, then spoke of "the church as a beautiful place in which to worship, until they should be called to that house, not made by hands, in the eternal heavens." Sam's fine voice then led the singing. He must have been like Ernie Bean in my days, of whom a lady in church said that she likes to sit next to him to hear him sing. I then warned her never to sit next to me.

In subsequent years, Sam's place was sold to one of the many Brown families here. Later his house burned; grass overgrew the ruins. I hiked on Sam's farmland, descending the hillside, and sometimes stumbled over his old foundation stones in the bottomland, until they also were removed for uninterrupted farming. There is no Sam Rude farm anymore, no trace of the family: "Its place remembers it no more." Nobody remembers him except for me, who never met him, my neighbor a hundred years ago.

Even experts on the physical world don't fully understand time, what it really is. Someone suggested time assures that not all events happen at once. One may add space assures that not all events happen at the same place. We know that collisions occur when objects meet simultaneously at the same spot. There may be conflicts of agreements among people at the same location, when their vital interests clash or coincide. I think I would have been quite agreeable with Sam Rude, representative of the many millions of worthy people nobody remembers, who are all known to God. "There where people sing happily, you may reside in peace. Evil people don't sing happy songs."[15]

---

15. Dad quotes this from "an old German song."

3. MIDFIELD TESTS
1930 – 1964

SHORT TEST REPORTS FROM THE MIDDLE OF

THE CENTURY IN GERMANY, WHICH PROVED TO

US THAT WE CAN CONFIDENTLY TRUST IN GOD.

THE CHICKADEES

"He must manage his own family well and see that his children obey him with proper respect."

—*1 Timothy 3:4*

During the course of the year, particularly in winter, we meet different families. The Blue Jays come to us, a very handsome family although somewhat on the noisy side. The Cardinals show up; apparently, a good Catholic family. Most frequent are the Chickadees. We did not know any of them in the old country or early on in America. Not until we moved from the suburbs to the Boonies would we become well acquainted. The Chickadees are my favorite family. Energetic little feather balls with beaks, they are always in good spirit, even in arctic winter weather. I have never met an unhappy Chickadee. They know how to live, while the heavenly father takes care of them. My folks in the old country were of spiritual kinship.

I joined them at home by the help of a midwife on a Sunday morning at eight o'clock.[16] Three sisters and two brothers welcomed me into our family. The next youngest sister[17] was eight years old and completely surprised by my arrival. Such was the state of communication in those days. My parents were in their mid-forties. Soon after birth, mother fell

---

16. Horst Wilfried Rauhut born May 4, 1930.
17. Hildegard—"Hilde" 5 Aug 1922 to 15 May 2009.

37

severely sick with a gall bladder infection. It was a life or death case. The doctor split the gall bladder, as was then customary. Mother's recovery took many months, while the baby [Horst] was taken care of by his oldest sister [Maria Anna = Aenne[18]] and mother's Christian friend and neighbor.

My father [Adolf Gustav, Sr.[19]] was an excellent, selfless provider and kept his house in order. My sisters introduced me to tiny meadow flowers and ducks on the pond. These are my earliest memories. One sister helped mother at home, often at the foot-pedaled sewing machine by the kitchen window. I played much in the kitchen, putting chairs together and a footstool on one of them, pretending to be a truck driver delivering merchandise. A Christian calendar was on the wall, from which we would tear and read daily messages, and a small, wooden tablet resembling an old scroll that said in German, "The debt certificate is torn. The payment is made. He has let me know that He set me free." I kept reading this message without comprehension, but now I remember it with understanding through the rest of the century.

Breakfast alternated between dislikes and likes. One morning I ate oatmeal porridge, the next morning I had rye bread and sugar-beet syrup, together with chocolate milk. I also remember a one-time special treat: a sweet roll with a piece of milk chocolate inside. It doesn't sound like much now. Then it was extraordinary. Shortly after seven in the evening, my oldest sister told me a bedtime story, usually from the Old Testament. These stories have lasted in my memory, in contrast to so many sermons later. Of course, she got tired of telling stories. So one night she resorted to talking about me instead. This did not go undetected, but while I protested I fell asleep.

I had joined a happy, caring, stable, Christian family, all this without

---

18. Maria Anna ("Aenne"; b: October 23, 1908; d November 25, 1979) Rauhut (m. Zimmermann and emigrated to Winnipeg, Canada.)

19. Adolf Gustav Rauhut (b: January 22, 1885, Steinwerder near Schildberg, Posen; d: July 23, 1945, Duesseldorf, Germany).

my own doing, and I did not know it any other way. Since then many nice people of various nationalities or ethnic groups have travelled with me or briefly walked my trail. While some could claim one or several of my family's attributes, few could claim them all. How fortunate I was becomes clear to me at this time when so many families fall apart, so many little children suffer and grow up undisciplined, unguided, exposed to countless, avoidable forms of misery.

THE HOUSE ASSOCIATION

"If it is possible, as far as it depends on you, live at peace with every-one."

—*Romans 12:18*

This house was home for decades. Therefore, a detailed description is in order. Built at the turn of the century by a Building & Savings Association, all tenants had shares in it, and rents were relatively low. The association owned many houses, twelve alone on our street. Our house had walls up to two feet thick, nine apartments on three floors, cellars for every tenant, a laundry room with old-fashioned washers, several rooms under the roof assigned to various apartments, an attic for drying cloth, and a top attic for a bird's eye view of the neighborhood.

Everything was spic and span, because the nine families of the house association took good care of all cleaning chores as detailed on circulating wooden tablets. These chores, carefully watched by all parties, included cleaning of cellar, stairways, house floors, and attic. First floor tenants also swept the sidewalk, shoveled snow, and cleaned all the doorbells with brass polish. We lived on the first floor on the right and regularly swept the sidewalk. However, this is not exclusively European, because the other day I saw a lady in America doing likewise, one lady out of more than one hundred million during the last thirty years.

I must have been three or four years old when I delivered milk to all tenants every morning, or so I pretended with an empty milk can while I preceded the real milkman. They all loved it and gave me candy in return. This went on for a long time, since both customers and vendor got what they expected. During many afternoons, I played in a neighbor's apartment upstairs, who took a long nap after lunch while I kept quiet. At four I woke her up asking whether I should get something from the baker. She usually consented and prepared coffee, which was first ground in a small coffee mill. Customarily, people enjoyed four meals a day including coffee and cake in the afternoon. Her real coffee tasted better than our substitute brand, pointed at both ends, which consisted of roasted barley. In the evening, her husband played on the mouth harmonica melancholic tunes, remindful of sad days during the Great War.

All tenants went regularly to church, to different churches, and many of them were committed Christians. They also helped each other. Dad carried coal from the cellar to the third floor apartment of an elderly lady, and I followed in his footsteps later. Thus, most of the time a good spirit prevailed in this house. If only the cleaning chores were not judged, or the standards not so close to perfection. For all shortcomings in floor cleaning or brass polishing could lead to unpleasant disagreements. Some effects of our work are always visible. It takes a combination of correction and forgiveness to live with each other, and always a shot of wisdom to choose the right response. Such are the challenges of communal life.

GARDEN MEMORIES

"Build houses and settle down; plant gardens and eat what they pro-
duce."

—*Jeremiah 29:5*

During the industrial revolution in the second half of the 1800s, Dr.
Schreber of Leipzig proposed gardens for people in the big cities. They
had come from rural areas and needed fresh air activities, he argued. The
idea spread like wild fire. Schreber Garden Associations were founded throughout Germany. Ours consisted of a main road, several smaller
ways branching from there, and the gardens in between. It also had a
place for refreshments, a bowling alley, a playground, tall privet hedges
on two sides, a railroad dam behind the bowling alley, and a fence separating the gardens from a soccer field. The gardens themselves covered
areas of about 10 by 25 meters. Each had a small cottage. My parents'
cottage included two low-ceiling rooms and even a toilet with flushing
water, proudly shown to all visitors. Father planted cherry, plum, pear,
and peach trees, red and black currents, gooseberry bushes, strawberries, vegetables, and many flowers, particularly long-stem tulips. Thus
he created a child's paradise, where mother would cheerfully squash ripe
strawberries onto buttered rye bread as a family treat.

The peach tree was grown from a big peach put into the ground. Seeing the apparent waste, I took the peach out of the ground and bit into

the ripe fruit, before my father buried it again. In due time, the tree provided many juicy peaches, including more than a hundred pounds during
the bitter post-war years of 1945-1947. The plum trees grew countless
pounds of the best plums. Cherries and pears were also quite good for
eating and canning in so-called Weck glasses with red rubber seals.

One day, father was painting a wooden bench light green. I watched
and told him where to paint, while he followed his own plans. Finally
he had enough of it and put me into my right place. So I learned to
leave a man alone when he is working, rather than giving unsolicited
advice. In front of our garden was a dark-green fence on a knee-high
concrete foundation, with a door in the middle and a padlock under a
rubber protective shield. Behind the fence in our compost pit ripened
rich, black organic fertilizer of horse and sheep manure. With its help
we grew king-size celery beets, later converted into delicious celery salad
after cleaning, cooking, cutting and combining them with oil, onions,
vinegar, salt and pepper. Horse apples and sheep droppings were hand-
picked with little shovels and carried in pails to the pit. Merchandise was
still distributed by horse-drawn vehicles before the war, and a herd of
sheep occasionally roamed through the vicinity. Thus, their fall-out was
of reasonable supply. To collect it was not below father's dignity, and it
should not have been below mine either. But whenever I helped I made
sure that no boys from our school would see my humble occupation.
Father claimed that even chicken would produce manure, but I cannot
remember that we ever got into this part of the business.

A great time was Gartenfest during summer, when hot dogs and
candies were offered by the association, and a tall pole was erected with
all kinds of goodies at the top including sausages and hams for climb-
ers to retrieve. Games, prizes and brass band music added to the excitement. Motor vehicles were seldom seen on the road nearby. A few
were three-wheelers; most unique was a compact two-seater nicknamed
"chaussee-louse" because of its shape. One could play safely on that road.
The hot black top invited me to draw water patterns on it with a leaky

milk can and see them disappear again. So it seems to be with many patterns of our transient lives. Our Schreber Garden Association is no more. It had to yield to the city's incinerator even before our immigration. We sold our garden in the fifties already, because mother was blind, I was at the university, and my sisters' families were too busy. For at least three decades, the garden served as an oasis of tranquility. It provided badly needed nourishment after the war. Happy memories and dreams remain.

TROUBLE IN PARADISE

"The heart is deceitful above all things and beyond cure. Who can understand it?"

—Jeremiah, 17:9

On hot summer days, father used to play the card game of Skat with two other men, one of them my friend Willi's father. They would sit at a little table in his garden, each drinking a bottle of beer, which was just "liquid bread" in their mindset and culture. But mother didn't like it. She said that the devil would sit under the table when men play cards. Curious, I lifted the tablecloth to see the devil under the table, but there was none. He would not show himself openly, but would deceive and influence the world of two small boys in his sinister ways.

Willi and I had little shovels. The ways to the gardens had received a new layer of black gravel. We put the two together and transferred some gravel to some gardens. Their owners complained immediately, and Willi got from his big mama the worst spanking I ever saw. I expected to be spanked next, but my father had seen Willi's treatment and was in no mood to repeat the scene.

Mother did not socialize much, but other women bowled and gave me the opportunity to make some money by putting up the pins and returning the bowling balls, which unlike the American variety had no finger holes. Thus I first experienced hard physical work around age ten.

Between the single-lane bowling alley and the railroad dam was our hideout for two years. There I smoked my first cigarette at the tender age of six with four other boys. Three Alfa cigarettes cost then five Pfennige, less than two cents. I never felt more miserable and immediately gave up smoking. However, I had a relapse at age eleven, when I turned to smoking peppermint tea from a white clay pipe. This ended when mother's friend, Aunt Else, watched me and destroyed the clay pipe on the ground. No wonder that I became a non-smoker.

Across from our garden was old Miss Althaus' small cottage, located close to her garden door. There was also Mr. Harnischmacher with his broad smile and Rhinish pitch. I remember one afternoon at the Althaus cottage in 1940, shortly after the Blitzkrieg against France, when he said: "The boys really showed them what they can do," and he puffed his pipe and filled the air with cheap tobacco smoke. Everybody agreed on that cloudy afternoon. Nobody foresaw the storm clouds soon to break loose over Germany with unprecedented force. The old souls of Althaus and Harnischmacher would not be around after another five years.

Not everything else was well either. Years earlier, perhaps at age six, I walked home from the garden, leaving my dad unaware that I had left. I was decorated with a sun visor and cracked-lens binoculars given to me by an aunt. A young man on a bicycle stopped and persuaded me to give him the binoculars in exchange for a cigar stump, which I declined. But when he requested to borrow them for a few days, I let them go, never to be seen again, my first disillusion with mankind.

ON WHEELS

"The crucible for silver and the fire for gold, but the LORD tests the hearts."

—Proverbs 17:3

As long as I can remember I see myself on wheels, by now approaching a million automobile miles after a humble beginning. The tricycle was exchanged for a very small bicycle at age four, followed by a boy's bike at six, and a regular size bike at eleven, all single-speed. The scooter came along at seven for the next five years. It was a fancy 'Wipproller' with stand-on lever mechanism to propel it without my feet touching the ground. All these early means of transportation were associated with Uncle Ernst, family and church friend, whose bike and repair shop was just fifteen walking minutes away from home.

I remember following our neighbors on my boy's bike, hardly being able to keep up with them. At seven or eight, I was riding with my classmate Bernd in the city forest. Racing down on a steeply sloped hiking trail, I suddenly realized that the end of the trail was an earth wall with steps for pedestrians. Quickly I turned my bike upward onto the wooded slope to my left. Like run-away trucks on an escape trail, we were saved from crashing. The scooter with its poor brakes got me also into trouble. When we rolled down on a busy street, a trolley car let out some passengers. Unfortunately, I bumped into a senior citizen walking with a cane, and all bystanders turned against me.

I liked to help uncle Ernst in his bicycle shop, so he asked me at age seven to assemble a few hundred little bolts, nuts, and washers. For this tedious job he paid me 157 Pfennige (copper pennies), the first money I ever made. Later I started to learn in his shop some valuable mechanical skills and to repair flat tires, waited on customers and handled the till of the store at age eleven. Uncle Ernst would sit in his shop by the stove, smoking his cigar during the afternoon coffee break. There was a drum with old paper I was carrying out to the garbage can. Coming back, I found to my surprise a new, wrinkled one-mark bill within the remaining paper. At once I gave it to him. Years later it dawned on me that this was a test. I still see his smiling face in apparent approval of my honesty.

He used to say: "This much business is better than this much work in the steel factory," comparing his pinky with his whole arm. In his sixties during the early war years, he would slowly walk home with a little lunch box containing the day's cash. He didn't deposit the money in the bank as required, but tried to hold on to it at home. However, he would lose it anyway, together with his multistory house, which was firebombed like most other city houses. But he retained his good heart, and I the pleasant memory that he introduced me to wheels.

EMMA HERMANNS

"May all who hate Zion be turned back in shame."

—Psalm 129:5

"The righteous hates what is false, but the wicked bring shame and disgrace."

—Proverbs 13:5

Two streets merged at an angle of forty—five degrees. At its corner was Emma Hermanns, a ladies garment store with three large display windows on both sides of the wedge-shaped house. Uncle Ernst was a family friend. One morning in 1938, I walked to his bike shop and saw that all Emma Hermanns windows were smashed. What happened? He would only mumble: "They did it." Thus I witnessed the day after the infamous "crystal night," so named after the smashed glass of Jewish properties and systematic burning of the synagogues. Later I asked myself why he did not speak up, since he was an otherwise outspoken critic and committed Christian. Perhaps caution and fear about his own store windows had gripped him.

One person from our church did speak up and landed in a concentration camp. When he got out temporarily and visited my mother, I heard him saying: "You know clearly what the communists are all about, but these people disguise themselves until you find out how they really are." The order for their misdeeds came from the top, while propaganda claimed it was a spontaneous reaction of the population. Witnesses report that the majority of the people remained silent, appalled, resigned, or indifferent. The majority of any nation does not consist of heroes. History describes frightening details of this event, which later led to the holocaust, the crime of the century, which is certainly not lacking crime or any inhumanity. Just a few years earlier, Jewish veterans had served in the Great War. My family had bought from Jewish merchants. Their doctors and teachers were appreciated. Not only glass, but also a sound world and delicate strings were broken. An evil monster was allowed to escape and would not be restrained until May of 1945. Ironically, so much glass was soon broken by bombing raids that the cities ran out of "crystal" and used translucent plastic sheets to cover their windows. "Who sows wind, will reap storm."

I thought about this subject often and long, read much of the literature and factual accounts. There is no rationale, only plain hatred. There are historical, economic, and political factors, and one reaches the conclusion that democracy, division of powers, and an independent system of justice are mandatory for society. Beyond that, the events make it very easy to believe in the existence of the devil, who kills and destroys, throws apart as in an explosive view. They also persuade us to seek the LORD, who taught us to pray: "Deliver us from the evil one." I marvel about the Bible's realism.

ON SUNDAYS

"I will instruct you and teach you the way you should go; I will counsel you and watch over you."

—*Psalm 32:8*

We went to a free church rather than a traditional church, either Protestant/Evangelical or Catholic. The gathering followed Mr. Darby from England, who must have planted it during the industrial revolution in the eighteen hundreds. I heard biblical stories at home and learned by heart such bible verses as John 3:16. As a four-year old I walked around the block, clockwise and counter-clockwise, reciting to myself this scripture of God's love. After so many years, it has been impossible to forget. A thirty minute walk led to Sunday school. I passed a street where church people lived with two little girls whom I was to escort for several years. Later I met them again as middle-aged ladies and reminded them of past services. They assured me that they would be forever grateful.

Sunday school was friendly teachers, happy songs, and bible stories. The total message and atmosphere had its impact and prepared me for a life-long church orientation. There were two church services, worship in the morning, and teachings in the afternoon, the latter one generally boring. Often I counted the glass panels in the high ceiling, except when an exciting speaker brought life into the congregation. All speakers were laymen. Their group rather than a single pastor took care of the services, and some did not believe in preparations.

During the Sunday school celebration at Christmas, children would recite verses and poems. They would be rewarded with cookies, candy, and fruit. I remember standing there, perhaps four years old, praising my parent's love in front of the full house and earning their applause. We also had a summer Sunday school picnic with games including sack races or balancing an egg on a spoon. Most people came by trolley car, but one beautiful family attracted our attention with their own automobile. Tragically, two of their daughters were to die of brain tumors after the war. One had become our very good friend and sister-in-law [Aunt Brigitte: married Magdalena's oldest brother Ernst, Jr.].

During the last two war years, I was evacuated to a quaint city [Halberstadt, Germany], where I attended Liebfrauen-Kirche. More than a thousand years old, originally a Catholic monastery, it became a Protestant church during the Reformation. There I was confirmed at fourteen by eighty-year old superintendent D. Lang. My confirmation verse from Psalm 32:8 was to become literally true in my life, as the good Lord has guided my steps in Germany and in America.

When we returned to our hometown and church after the war, I was belatedly baptized, which had to be done in a suburban bathtub, since all other options, including inner-city bathtubs, were destroyed by bombs. Baptism committed me, but my faith was like a flickering candle and lacked much understanding. Not until age twenty-two did I learn that we are saved by grace and not through our good works, which never seemed to accumulate anyway.

OBSERVATIONS ON VACATIONS

You know how to interpret the appearance of the sky, but you cannot interpret the signs of the times.

—Matthew 16:3

My father's employer [Henkel] was unusually social-minded. Among the services for their employees' families was a children's vacation plan. Brother, sister, and I benefitted from it several times. At age seven, I was sent to the Harz Mountains, at nine to the Luneburg Heath, and at eleven to the hilly land near Wiehl, three memorable vacations otherwise not experienced during the Great Depression. The company had their own health department. A doctor and a professional nurse examined the children. I remember that the doctor asked me to jump on a small table at seven. Boys and girls were given clothing and shoes from the company, Bavarian style shorts for the boys, and Dirndl dresses for the girls. Then off they went by train for four to six weeks.

The spacious place in the Harz Mountains was professionally run. Upstairs were the sleeping halls, downstairs the dining hall and play area in a small yard behind the building, with mountains all around. I remember looking through the dining hall window onto blue-colored, elevated features in the background. I wondered what they might be. Never before had I seen wooded mountains. Before long, we took walks there, saw the sheer rock formation not far from the house, and visited a sunny hillside meadow. Then we somersaulted on the grass, which resulted in green stains on my light shirt. It was a friendly village with a unique monument and many flowers. Sunny, happy images still remain in my mind. When I came home I wondered why the city and sky looked so grey.

We went to the country house in Luneberg by train and bus, through the flat, cloudy, heath landscape in northern Germany. White sand almost up to the surface, low fir trees, a large yard with some tall oaks. Not far from the house was a small hill from where the boys jumped far into the sand below, supported by a tall poll. It was in the beginning of September, 1939. Our young lady supervisor told us one evening that war has broken out, and she suppressed some tears. What did we know? Perhaps it would not break out after all. Contrary to any propaganda, it was not popular news. Cloudy skies were over us when we left for home, where I tried to persuade my playmates that war was a bad idea, as if it was still an option.

When I went on my summer vacation in 1941, war was already in full swing, but we were still spared. Some rain, some shine, a country house of the Evangelical Church, a custodian couple, and some supervising ladies for the children. Swimming in the outdoor pool of Wiehl, picking blueberries in the woods, helping farmers with their hay, playing in the creek, walking on the hillside, such were our activities. The boys cornered and killed a poisonous snake.

The population was made aware of air raids and phosphorus bombs. One was ignited by forcefully throwing it to the ground. We went home from a swim at sunny noontime of a beautiful day. Soldiers marched on a cross road, in front an officer on horseback. The horse danced, officer and soldiers got attention, our young lady smiled as they marched on. A flicker of time, and an unseen mirror reflected a trail of tears and death in fading light.

WHEN WHITSUNDAY TURNED RED

"Watch out! Be on your guard against all kinds of greed; a man's life does not consist in the abundance of his possessions."

—*Luke 12:15*

A major air raid on our city [Düsseldorf] occurred on June 12, 1943, during the night from Friday to Saturday. The following day was Pentecost. Cakes were baked and houses decorated. Mother's sister Maria had come from the Bremen area. Friday night I was riding my bike home, going straight west, when I saw the most intense and beautiful, red evening sky. As if the city was on fire, I thought, not anticipating an equally red but smoky sky one day later.

The house association was huddled in a cellar room selected for most likely survival. There were bunk beds for the children, but I chose to peek out of the house door and saw a noisy scenario of airplanes tracked by giant light beams, fires reflected in the sky, and smoke moving through the street. Neighbor Roettges, a Great War veteran, pulled me inside: "You are too young to die." Miss Puetz prayed: "Oh God, if you get me out of this situation, I'll always do what is right" (HE did, she didn't.). Aunt Maria stayed remarkably calm, sustained by unwavering faith.

In case we should be buried under rubble, the families agreed to open a passage to the next house, which was closed by bricks inside a heavy concrete wall. It was easily opened with a pickax. Meanwhile the roof burned, the fire caused by an octagonal phosphorus bomb, about twenty inches long. Most German cities succumbed to such giant matches. Fortunately, father was home. As fireman at Henkel Chemicals, he worked twenty-four-hour shifts, then he came home for the same length of time. With skill he organized a bucket chain and fought the fire, while the air raid raged and a flier shot from the air. At the end, father and the house association succeeded in saving the house, but the next three houses up to the street corner and across the street slowly burned to the ground, story by story. A smoky Saturday morning dawned. Some neighbors had saved and stored their furniture in the middle of the street. The lower floors of their five-story house were still burning, when the huge brick gable, unstable without its structural support, slowly tilted and fell onto the street, smashing beds, tables, chairs, and cabinets. Someone yelled and warned the bystanders in time, so nobody was hurt.

Mr. Armbrecht owned the burning house and grocery store next door. A gateway served as a garage for his two-seated Auto-Union car, which was removed before the flames got to it. When the ceiling over his store collapsed and his merchandise began to burn, he collapsed, too. Neighbors caught him before he touched the ground. To see the fiery end of his possessions was too much for our wealthy neighbor. Later, after an air raid on a quaint city, I observed another man breaking down in view of the destruction of his property. Not so Magdalena's Christian parents, who lost everything in June of 1943. Of course, there is a link between loss and grief, between war and poverty. Yet if the war taught us anything, it is not to be attached to material things, which no one can keep anyway.

OF SNAILS AND SCHOOL BOYS

"You will not fear the terror of night, nor the arrow that flies by day."

—*Psalm 91:5*

Even though our house was saved from total destruction, its upper floor was partially gutted and its roof was partially gone. My own room under the roof was spared. It contained among other treasures a large jar used as an aquarium for one fish, three snails, and several tadpoles. A piece of mortar had fallen into the water, and everybody inside was dead. I hated this sight wholeheartedly, more so than all other destruction around me.

Our roof consisted of overlapping brick shingles on a wooden lattice structure. Explosions had caused many shingles to fall and shatter on the ground. Some large bombs had penetrated houses, including a corner house in the neighborhood, where one went through five floors before it exploded and killed all residents in the cellar. A few days later, I helped fix our roof by consolidating remaining and new shingles. I was sitting on the lattice structure and enjoyed my lofty vantage point, more than four stories high. Suddenly a bomb exploded (either by time fuse or accident). Shock and fright could have thrown me off the roof, but both came and went so fast that I didn't know which way to fall and was still sitting on the same spot when it was over. I decided that I would probably stay that way, and lived to tell the story.

The air war had started by sporadic bombing in 1940. Then everybody went out in curiosity to see the damage. This was no longer necessary in subsequent years. The winter of 1941 to 1942 was extremely cold. Since coal had to be saved, schools were closed for several weeks, and we received lengthy homework assignments. Meanwhile more bombs fell on the city during the nights. One morning I learned in school that classmate Horst Hamm and family were killed by a bomb, which also destroyed his father's butcher shop near the station. Nice boy, same first name, birthday, year of birth, dead at twelve, while I was spared. I'll not attempt to explain tragedy. After so many years, I am now reminded of "the eighteen who died when the tower of Siloam fell on them" two thousand years ago, a tragedy not explained either.

The first major air raid on our city [Düsseldorf] occurred on August 1, 1942. It gutted the old city core, a place with city rights since 1288. We went to see the mess with sister Klara and her friend Martha, who was in a nurse's uniform. There was this youth, his face blackened by smoke, who helped the victims. She recognized his hero image. He recognized her admiring looks. Both felt acknowledged at a time when heroism was in. They overlooked the fact that stupidity was also in, with war being waged on their and other peoples' backs.

The June 1943 air attack had a major personal impact. Only once more, in April 1945, did I experience such a close call. Besides, our city was declared an evacuation zone for children, and I had to leave the place where I was born. For the next six weeks, I went to the East and stayed on Aunt Bela's farm. From there I came to a quaint city at the Harz Mountains for the rest of the war.

A LADY OF FAITH

"The LORD gave, and the LORD has taken away; blessed be the name of the LORD."

—*Job 1:21*

The War had profound effects on our family. As I detail the trail of tragic events, I start in 1940. Mother was very sick and became blind. Cataract was then not easily operated on or free of risks; the professor could not guarantee a successful operation. While she still had some light versus dark sensation, she hesitated and decided against surgery. As time progressed, her eyes further deteriorated. Then she received the official word that her oldest son [Adolf, Jr.] was killed in Ukraine on July 23, 1941, and buried westward of Kiev. A strongly Christian boy of 24, he was very close to mother and the whole family. As we pondered the sad news during breakfast on a sunny summer morning, our family named him most precious, and thus he was mourned in his obituary. In his last diary entry on July 21, 1941, we read: "Peace I leave with you. My peace I give you. This word spoke to my heart today." Months later, a wounded soldier visited us and told mother in my presence that my brother had tried to rescue him, but was mortally hit. The dead and the wounded spent two hours together on Ukrainian soil before they were found.

In 1942, my second brother [Helmut] was seriously wounded by a shot through his neck in the bitter Russian winter campaign. He was sent to the Hohentwiel area south of the Black Forest. Mother and sister Anne [Maria Anne] visited him there. After he recuperated at home, he got engaged to a young lady from the church. I spent some time with them visiting people. When we visited their mutual friends in suburbia, they talked politics, in particular about postwar Germany after a lost war. As they were weighing several scenarios, they felt that the Catholic Church would become the dominant political factor, and this actually happened later in the Rhineland. Then they spotted me listening in curiosity, and I was warned: "You, with your big ears, keep that for yourself." So I did not tell the tale until now. Otherwise, we all would have been in deep trouble with the secret police, who did not tolerate any defeatist attitude. We know now that many people were executed for nonconformity with propaganda phrases. My brother was sent again to Russia and became MIA (missing in action) in the fall of 1943. No further information became available, but mother saw him later in a vision, in a POW camp with his tin dish of soup, sad-faced and apologetic about any grief he may have caused her. A fine, athletic, frustrated boy, one of many millions wasted.

Herbert became sister Hildegard's fiancé, a young bright-eyed lieutenant, Christian friend of my brothers, with whom they enjoyed many occasions of swimming in the pool and on the beach. They tolerated me as a little brother, although my presence, strictly speaking, was unnecessary. Herbert died by a partisan shot through his head.

My sister Klara died instantly, just before the end of the war. Four days after her March 23rd birthday, she walked to our home from the church house for unwed mothers, where she was employed as a social nurse. One block away from home, she was hit by artillery. The Allies on the west bank of the Rhine were then shelling the power station in our area. Since no ordinary funeral was possible under artillery attack, she was buried in the yard of the church house by fellow social nurses. Trained as a surgery-nurse in northern Germany, she had transferred to social services. She belonged to the Berlin-Zehlendorf sorority of deaconesses of the Evangelical Church, who published her and other nurses' eulogies. A most gentle person, I still see the quiet sadness in her eyes, when we were sitting on top of mountain rocks near the quaint city in 1944. One day before or after March 27, 1945, father was hit by artillery at work, was seriously wounded in his thigh, developed gangrene, and died in the local hospital after the war, on the same day as his oldest boy died four years earlier. Since there was no mail or other communication, I learned about my sister's death and father's injury when I came home by bike in June of 1945. My young sister [Hilde] and I were with him when he died, the name of Jesus on his lips, but mother and sister Anne did not get the sad message until fall of that tragic year.

This concluded our family's trail of tears. Only the soldier, and the civilian at the receiving end of war, may fully relate to its reality. Yet, through it all, barely audible, rang a gentle tune of peace and faith, with far reaching consequences.

Düsseldorf intersection of Höherweg & Kettwiger Strasse where Tante Kläre was killed by artillery on 27 April 1945. Visited 16 August 2019

A LADY OF FAITH

She met tragedies without complaining.
One year she lost her eyesight,
next year, she lost her son,
two years later her second son,
the following year her son-in-law,
after one year, two loved ones,
her daughter and her husband.

Reminds you of Job?
Good grief, without visual distraction.
When the final blow fell,
she responded by praising the LORD,
not cynical, not bitter.
Conceded: each blow went through her heart

How do I know her story,
report it correctly?
I knew her quite well.
She was my mother.
Her inner strength
and example persuaded me
to follow her path of trust,
her confident life.
Notable lady of faith.

AUNT BELA'S[20] FARM

"Keep your lives free from the love of money and be content with what you have, because God has said, "Never will I leave you; never will I forsake you."

—Hebrews 13:5

During summer time in 1942 and 1943, I visited Aunt Bela's farm in the East. This was Polish territory between the two world wars and has been Polish again since the end of the second war. Earlier it belonged to an eastern Prussian province [Duchy of Posen]. Both Polish and German was spoken in this border region. All locations have Polish names now, which are unfamiliar to me. Germans and Poles lived in this area for centuries. Dad [Adolf Gustav] and I traveled by train via Berlin, where we stayed with relatives and saw the sights of this city before they were destroyed. We continued our journey beyond Frankfurt on the Oder

---

20. Dad's mother, Johanna Klose, had six siblings; Johann, Karoline, Thomas, Maria, Karl, and Berta. I believe when Dad refers to Aunt Bela he means Aunt Berta.

River. My uncle and Aunt Bela [Richard and Berta Gabriel[21]] picked us up by horse and wagon and for one and a half hours towed us over almost flat terrain to their farm.

There were recurring chores, such as watching the cows so that they would not stray into adjacent wheat fields. Anna, a kind Polish girl, perhaps four years older than I, watched the neighbor's cows. We talked, and when I mentioned the bombing raids on German cities, her eyes gleamed. How much suffering and injustice her people must have endured, that she drew hope from other people's suffering. Toward me was no hostility. Other chores and events included helping to build a new brick stable, helping with the harvest, going to the water-driven mill, swimming and boating in the mill pond and river, and bicycle riding. Once I rode my bike to get butter on ration stamps. Polish women went to town, walking barefoot for hours, their shoes in their hands. I had to stand in line among them. Not understanding one word, I missed being served for many hours.

Several relatives remembered Aunt Bela's farm with its good food supply during those frugal war years. They came from northern Germany and from Silesia. An old uncle and I visited one of his Polish friends on a warm Sunday. Resting on the grass behind a barn, they shared for hours in the Polish language. Excluded from the conversation, I took a grass blade and occasionally tickled uncle's neck. He thought it was a fly, but never caught it or me.

Dad took me by bike to his family's farmhouse, where grandma overwhelmed us with her hospitality. It took about two hours to get to her

---

21. Johanna Klose's youngest sister, Berta ("Aunt Bela") Klose, married Richard Gabriel and had three sons, Richard, Helmut, and Herbert. This family plus two additional children escaped Russian troops at the end of 1944 and went to the Halberstadt area just short of the later Iron Curtain. They settled in the village of Anderbeck. The farm help loaded up the family (minus Richard away serving as a soldier) in a wagon pulled by two horses. Richard (a P.O.W.) was upset when he reunited that his wife didn't take refuge in the west. They lived in East Germany. We believe the eldest son Ernst became a high-ranking Stasi officer (Colonel).

modest farm. The area's landscape was reflected deep within me. I felt close kinship and distant space, not experienced again until I came to America. There were our old family ties, yet I was separated. There was space, connecting places where family had lived and died. There was a vast blue sky and brisk air, sometimes quite cold in August. The term "Cold Homeland' is descriptive. You came into the kitchen with its trough of sour dough. Formed into loaves of dark rye bread, they were baked in a wood-heated tile oven. Twigs were put into the baking space. A brown crust formed on the round loaf that was served with fresh butter. It all had an unforgettable odor and taste. Potatoes were peeled in the evening, and everybody dipped into the same bowl of sour cream.

One beautiful summer afternoon, Dad took me to friend Olga's farm. She did not expect us, was delighted, and immediately baked a huge streusel cake with many eggs. It was a perfect afternoon of happy fellowship. A neighbor drove by at a quick pace, standing in his wagon, directing his horse. They talked about him. To me his appearance and disappearance was like a phantom. Thus, our happiness would disappear, too. In short order, during the bitter winter of 1944/1945, Olga struggled westward through the snow, barely ahead of pursuing Russian soldiers.

Aunt Bela's farm intrigued my sense of history and facts at age thirteen already, and so I will just briefly tell the rest of the story. Her farm was not really hers. It belonged to a Polish farmer who lost it. My uncle [Richard Gabriel] was greedy enough to take advantage of the situation by exchanging the sandy place of Bela's original farm for a much nicer one with rich soil. That may be the reason why he discouraged me to see mother's family place and cemetery in another small village. Perhaps because of a bad conscience, they occasionally sent their Polish maid with food to the original owner in the deep woods and bought berries from him in return. I am glad that Dad's family stayed on their modest farm. The Polish people appreciated and remembered them with respect, and even took care of Grandpa's grave [Andreas Johann Rauhut], as witnessed by visiting relatives.

There is an epilogue. Aunt Bela lost everything but a few possessions, horse and wagon, with which her family and a Polish helper arrived near the quaint city in early 1945. The maid chose to stay behind. My uncle returned late from a Russian prisoner of war camp, to find his family in communist East Germany, only a few miles away from the more pleasant West. Almost all Germans were expelled from Polish territory. But that turned out to be a blessing in disguise. Many Polish people later tried to get into prosperous Western Europe. The cycle of justice and injustice never ceases because of continuing human mismanagement and selfishness.

As for me, I left the area on August 27, 1943 at 1 PM, to arrive in Berlin at 9 PM. Kaiserallee street was dark; the house had burned down a few nights ago. My relatives lived in a garage and did not hear me coming. I had a hard time forcing my body through the bars of their wrought-iron fence. The next day saw me in the quaint city, where I attended school for the rest of the war.

OUT OF THE BLUE SKY

"I will save you. You will not fall by the sword but escape with your life, because you trust in me."

—Jeremiah 39:18

Thanks goodness, the war came to an end and quicker than we thought. We grew sick of nightly alarms, going to air raid shelters and losing sleep. Day and night, bombers flew over us to pulverize Berlin. Unchallenged, they flew in tight formation through the blue spring sky, as widely spread as one could see in a viewing section. The great tragedy of Dresden occurred only a few weeks before the end. Packed with refugees, the city is said to have suffered more casualties than Hiroshima and Nagasaki combined. In 1944, we still witnessed fighter action, most dramatically when the ball bearing factory in southern Germany was attacked and significant numbers of Allied bombers were shot down in our vicinity.

I went by bike from the quaint city [Halberstadt] to visit my cousin at the southern edge of the Harz Mountains, a day trip over empty roads where I met only one person. On the way back, I experienced a scary moment when a German fighter plane brushed the tree top over me, pursued by an Allied fighter plane which brushed that tree top seconds later. Then the German plane burned and tumbled to the ground.

The end of the war appears strangely inconsistent. I remember soldiers on leave displaying their uniforms on the quaint city's business street in a curiously tough and idle atmosphere in contrast to the Total War propaganda, as if dying and scrambling at the front had become irrelevant. The same atmosphere prevailed elsewhere; military officers and enlisted men gave the cynical impression that everything was safe and sound. Then came the refugees from the Aachen area, which was liberated by American troops in October 1944.

Then came the time of misled idealism. One classmate opted to defend Berlin and to die at the tender age of fourteen. A young veteran with one arm, one leg, a decorated chest between the two, and single-minded conviction of official propaganda tried to mislead fifteen-year old boys against enemy tanks. One time, the whole school body was put into an auditorium, where some recruiting officers presented propaganda. Thereafter, every fifteen-year old boy had to "volunteer" for armed service. Not conviction, but force put many on the line. How did I get out of these traps? I was only fourteen.

There were other dangers as well. My mood was sad, since two brothers had died already. Was dying not also my destination? When I saw the end approaching, I mentioned to classmates that the war might be lost. Answered one of them: "If that should happen, it is because of people like you." My skeptical remark could have caused trouble, even death for spreading rumors. In fact, I was warned by someone else, who knew my family, that our names would be included in a city card index of ideologically unreliable persons.

Three days before liberating the quaint city in 1945, the Allies burnt it into a heap of ashes. The officials would not give in, and the Allies wanted to avoid any casualties. At Sunday noon on April 8, we walked home from church in brisk air and sunshine. Looking south into the sun, we saw waves of Allied airplanes approaching and bombing the city out of the blue sky. There was no air defense. We lived on the most northern street and would be hit last it seemed. Behind us there was a park, then fields. The old house had no basement, only a brick tunnel two steps below ground. There my aunt, my mother, and other women were seeking shelter. Running through the garden into the park to watch the events, I rested briefly under a ball tree, briefly enough to escape the unexploded bomb that hit the vicinity minutes later. The city burned for days, then smoldered and calmed down. Our street was spared.

Eerie silence fell over the city in the afternoon before its pending occupation. American tanks came slowly to the northwestern entrance, preceded by soldiers with walkie-talkies, neat uniforms, and clean boots. Methodically they moved forward without a fight. The local end phase of the war had tapered down to the chore of occupying open land. A jolly young soldier with the neat appearance of a midwestern farm boy came to our door. Friendly enough to expect an invitation to America, he asked me instead whether there were soldiers in the house. I answered in English that there were none. People put white flags into the windows, no hostility on either side discernable. A joyous atmosphere of relief flooded the street. During the following days, government food storage areas were looted by Germans and foreign workers alike. For weeks, an easy calm prevailed. No school would distract us. Sunny days were filled with swimming and relaxing, until the reality of postwar Germany set in.

One episode on the day of occupation I must mention, since it could have made the rest of my story obsolete. In late evening I was careless enough to venture through the garden gate behind our house into the adjacent park, not knowing that it served as campground for an American army unit. It was very dark. Three sentries in different locations noticed someone coming and called each other or perhaps me. Finally, I stood still, when one of the soldiers approached me with his raised rifle and a flashlight, then let me go. If the visibility of their target would have been better, or if they would have been more trigger-happy, they could have easily prevented my future immigration to America.

SWISS CHEESE PLUS JEWELRY

"Would it not be better for you to be wronged? Would it not be better for you to be robbed?"

— 1 Corinthians 6:7

This story reflects on the transitory nature of our possessions and on our reluctance to let go. It also describes a case of highway robbery, when no laws were in effect or enforceable. The time frame was June-July of 1945. A wheel of Swiss cheese and a bag of jewelry attracted my attention at the quaint city, following other dramatic events.

In mid-June, a family friend and I rode our bikes from the quaint city to our homes on the Rhine, a distance of about 350 Kilometers. We headed around the Harz Mountains towards the Weser River, where acquaintances granted us lodging for one night. An American patrol checked us but let us pass. Further west, we could take a train for a while, followed by another bike ride, train, and final bike transportation. Railroads were then interrupted through massive bridge destructions. I almost didn't reach my destination. My bike and I had taken lofty positions on top of a railroad car, when several low signal bridges appeared in short succession, which would have killed or hit me hard. By quickly ducking could I retain my head. The good LORD had His hand in avoiding the accident, as he let me look forward at the right time rather than back. After a few days I was home. House and apartment still existed. Aunt Else had defended the latter against folks who looked for empty apartments in our bombed-out city. There I learned about my sister's death and visited my dad in the hospital, before I became a messenger of tragedy on my way back to mom and two sisters in the quaint city. Some people gave me letters for loved ones located in the middle of Germany, since there was no other means of communication. Thus, temporary and unofficially, I became a mail man, too. I was able to fetch a truck ride and then pedaled the final stretch by bike. Delivering the letters was not without challenges because of marauding people, who forcefully took bikes away from unwary travelers. Only by hanging on to the rear of a speeding truck did I keep mine.

As mentioned earlier, the quaint city was first occupied by American troops. When they moved on, the British moved in. But British troops were to leave, too, in accordance with the Treaty of Yalta, which awarded the former Soviet Union with a major portion of Germany conquered by the western allies. During that time in early July, a man from our home town sent a truck for his very pregnant daughter in the quaint city, and my youngest sister could join her on the way home. Our father was dying, but his condition remained unknown to us in the quaint city, since telephone, telegram or mail services were unavailable.

Meanwhile, the Soviets began to occupy the quaint city with their Panje wagons, one horse per wagon. My mother and oldest sister were now quite anxious to get out and take me home to the Rhineland.

We have to digress now and introduce Mrs. Run, a refugee lady from the Oder River area. There was a sympathetic openness in her eyes, but I would not describe her as a southern belle. Inconspicuous in the quaint city until its military occupation, she effectively served her interests immediately thereafter. We first noticed her when she rolled a wheel-size Swiss cheese into the house. I didn't know where she got it. In fact, I didn't even know this kind of cheese in any form other than a small slither. Then in short order she had a car, bikes, a truck, and she was determined to go west and away from the Soviets. That became our common denominator. The loaded truck waited for us at a farm just a few miles down the road in the next village. But the British let nobody pass until the Soviets were in the city. This would not deter Mrs. Run, who would solve this problem relatively quickly with a bottle of Schnapps.

At noon time at the farm house, two high Soviet officers stopped their limousine, politely asked for lunch, and sat down in the dining room. At that time, Mrs. Run decided to pick up something she forgot in the quaint city and asked me to accompany her. So we were riding our bikes down the road again, when several wild people suddenly stormed toward us to rob our bikes. Since we resisted, they used brute force. One of them took a big stick, swung it high over his head and let it come down to separate my hand from the handlebar. Anticipating the blow, I yielded the bike in the nick of time and avoided a broken wrist. But the lady continued to resist her assailant. Without stick, he wrestled the bike away from her, then took her purse from the handlebar and threw it to her, probably thinking it would contain a hanky or two, next to a vast collection of vanity items occasionally found in a lady's purse. However, it was loaded with jewelry. This episode was the only positive thing about our experience with highway robbery and about our first, unsuccessful attempt to escape from the Soviet occupation zone. It was not the last one.

HOME COMING

"There are many homes up there where my Father lives and I am going to prepare them for your coming."

—*John 14:2*

A few days after my ill-fated bike ride, a classmate invited me to join him and some Italian friends on a successful western excursion. By train we went to a small village, then pulled a cart with our luggage through the sunny woods to the foothills of the Harz Mountains. This was a wonderful hike, one of those you wish would last forever. The area was not yet taken over by Soviet troops, and the poor residents did not anticipate their imminent fate of becoming pawns of a communist empire. A truck gave us a rough ride along the spine of the Harz Mountains to an area under American control. There we spent one Sunday swimming, cooking, and eating, before taking a train westward on the next day. We slept in an empty railroad car. Finally, at home I joined my youngest sister, one week before our father died.

He died slowly, like an extinguishing candle, at peace with our LORD. In the morning, a neighbor had begged me to deliver a wreath to the cemetery for her husband's funeral. It was an omen for more death to arrive. On a sunny, hot day in July, we buried dad and our sister Klara together in one large grave. It was her final resting place after the assignment of a temporary one in a back yard during the artillery bombardment. Many people attended the graveside service and showed their compassion, while mother and our oldest sister in the quaint city were unaware of these events. We walked home with one of our cousins on this hot afternoon. At home, family and friends commemorated the dead and sang the family's favorite song, "Great God, We Praise You," so hard to understand by most people in similar circumstances. That evening, it occurred to me that I had become the family's sole male descendant. My response was sudden, unnecessary action, putting small nails and screws of father's tool box in order, perhaps as a mandate to put our house in order after receiving so many blows from the now silent war machine. Emotions and tears would have been right, but public fears postponed them till night, when I was alone, quite quiet.

A conditioning of the heart is available to those whom the LORD grants it. That was mom's case before she received the sad news by messenger in autumn. A Christian lady of happy persuasion had stayed with her for weeks, and they sang songs of praise, which softened the blow, which still hit hard. As she revealed later in Maryland, she thought she would never laugh again. But hearty laughs we shared already in Europe. My oldest sister and mom were reunited with us in October of 1945. By that time the iron curtain started to become less porous. Soviet soldiers patrolled the border between East and West. Mom and sister had to wade through a swamp like storks. A soldier was interested in mom's fur collar, but my sister protested so strongly that he let her keep it. Thus, they reached our home, home at last, yet of their past.

OPPORTUNITIES THROUGH HUNGER

"They were hungry and thirsty, and their lives ebbed away. Then they cried out to the Lord in their trouble, and He delivered them from their distress. Let them give thanks to the Lord for His unfailing love and His wonderful deeds for men."

—Psalm 107: 5, 6, 8

When you are young and hungry, you would work for a sandwich. Right after the war, city residents suffered from hunger and cold. Food was rationed but was largely non-existent. On an old bike with one tire on the rear wheel and full rubber in the front, I rode to a farm on the rolling hills above the river. At mid-morning I arrived and asked for work. The farmer had already enough help, said no, and left. When he had left, I took the next fork and put hay into the stable. Since I worked, I ate lunch. Since I had lunch, I was obliged to work. Since I worked, I was entitled to supper. Because I was not out, I was in. Persistence pays. Thus I started my summer employment on the farm, which grew mainly vegetables, potatoes, and grass to make hay.

I got involved in all kinds of operations, by hand and by horse. They had big Belgian horses for their two-wheel carts. Occasionally, horseshoes were needed, and I was riding to the blacksmith. One Saturday afternoon, I was smoothing the soil with a big roller. Chains were hitched to the horse. After the job was done in early evening, I took horse and roller down to the farm house and stable, situated at a lower plateau. I realized that the horse could not hold back the chain-drawn roller, which would accelerate by gravity. Therefore, as the roller continued to accelerate, I made the horse run faster and faster. With great noise, horse, roller and I made it safely to the farm. The horse should have had some self-interest as the roller could have hit its rear legs, but it did not understand the laws of gravity. So we got a lot of attention, the windows opened quickly, and everybody asked: "Who is coming with such tremendous noise? Why did you not leave the roller on the field?"

When school started, I worked only on Saturdays and during vacation. One time I went home with a fifty-pound green pumpkin, which I had to balance between the handlebar of the bike and my body. This worked all right, as long as I was bike riding. But when I had to walk the bike at a shortcut, the pumpkin rolled off and downhill. It took quite an effort to catch up with it and get it home, where the family used a sweet and sour recipe to preserve it.

The farmer was now ready to pay me. But money was without value, and we agreed that he would pay me with vegetables, essentially with a hand cart full of red beets. Thus, I became provider of the family, while my oldest sister served as great home economist with our meager rations. Breakfast consisted of one thin slice of black full-grain rye bread with a sandwich spread cooked of yeast, water, and some caraway seed. This was amended by a few slices of red beets, one morning served cooked, another morning served raw. We never felt full, and in hindsight, this was a most nourishing breakfast, full of minerals and vitamins A, B, and C.

There was a potato field on the farm, opened to city dwellers for gleaning on the morning after harvest day. We walked up there before dawn, pulling a handcart, with our friendly family doctor. When we arrived in the dark, the field was already crowded with hungry people. Mounted police kept order. At a given moment, the field was given free, and everybody hustled to get a small share of leftover potatoes. Such were the days when hunger and cold prevailed. But hearts were warm and our family was happy, even though only four of us out of eight were left.

We got the monthly butter ration, about the size of one of those portions we might see at a restaurant breakfast today. So we asked ourselves whether we should eat it piecemeal or at once. We decided to indulge in luxury and made a buttercream tort. For once, we lived really well.

Another time, we received about a dozen sugar beets, used in the Rhineland to make delicious sugar beet syrup. We cleaned, cooked, and pressed these beets, then condensed the juice. There was substantial leftover pulp, too valuable to discard, it seemed. So we put it into a pan for pancakes. The trouble was that we had no grease except for traces of bacon on an old, brown pigskin. Those pancakes of cellulose were the hardest things we ever tried to digest.

Students at school got a daily portion of vitamin C and also soup. We received somewhat rancid pea soup, but one day per week delicious biscuit soup. The pea soup was sometimes so bad that a whole pail was left over. I remember taking one pail home, walking with it for forty-five minutes through the city. Our family was thankful for everything. In those years, a family named Fereira from South Africa sent us two parcels of real flour through the church. Another kind church family provided occasionally a little sheep fat. Such acts of kindness cannot be forgotten. Fat was particularly scarce. Of course, a fatless diet was healthy for everyone. Later I met a medical doctor who stated that in those years cases of heart attack were unknown but came back quickly when people started to live "better."

Then came the fall day when I was hiking home with a little metal case containing bacon for my sister's birthday in October. I had saved it from several farm sandwiches served on Saturday nights only. My happiness and her appreciation for such [a] valuable gift were never surpassed. I am glad that I experienced those difficult years, which taught us gratitude for our daily bread. Up to this day, we do not take it for granted. Regarding thankfulness, we were given and gladly accepted opportunities of German and American church organizations to help the hungry in this world. Our children had to finish the food on their plates. It would not be thrown away. When one of their young friends was asked to do likewise, objected, and remarked that a food shortage would never happen in America, I answered, "Don't be so sure. I have seen very strange things happen."

MORE THAN A DOCTOR

"He who walks with the wise grows wise, but a companion of fools suffers harm"

—*Proverbs 13:20*

My sister, a nurse, made the doctor's acquaintance during the war, when both served as medical assistants in air raid shelters. After the war, she became our family physician and took a special interest in us, since my sister had died by artillery fire on our city in 1945. Soon I became one of her patients for minor afflictions, such as colds and flu. She took time for me, and we always talked after a brief medical examination and her writing my prescriptions. In due course, she became my counselor and motherly friend. Thereby, she exerted a significant influence on me during my formative years. So many diverse things I remember as a student, that only she could tell. She was a lady of deep thought and faith, knowledgeable and wise, and yet pragmatic.

She was far ahead of the medical community in recognizing essential factors of healthy living. Fifty years ago already, she recommended fibers in our diet, bran, much vegetable and water consumption, together with other healthy practices of the great Swedish dietician Waerland, then in his eighties, who used to ride his bicycle on steep German country roads, at a time when bicycles had only one hard gear. She taught the merits of long walking for physical and mental well-being, way before you could see the now frequent groups of senior citizens on our streets and in our shopping centers. In her faith and thinking she was absolutely positive, like Norman Vincent Peale. She realized that people may practice different variants of our Christian faith, from the very simple to the sophisticated. In this context she praised my mother's simple, steadfast faith, which was proven and unshaken in the fire of life's hardest tests. For all her goodness, I had the opportunity to take care of her, too, in practical ways, for instance in the fall of 1946, when I notified her that potatoes could be "gleaned" at a farm early in the morning. We walked up there together in the dark for two hours around 5 am, pulling an empty hand-wagon behind us. It got only partially filled with the precious earthly yield, which we then shared during those hunger years.

We don't know much about the doctor's private life, other than that she was a caring person to her older sister, and that she was married at one time and had a son, but I don't know whether he was naturally her own. Would she reconsider marriage? She was skeptical, but conceded that happy marriages are possible. At that time I got engaged to your mother. "Let me see her photo," she demanded, then looked into the girl's eyes with a magnifying glass. "You can tell by the eyes what kind of person she is." I was relieved when your mother passed the test.

The doctor, a devout member of her evangelical (traditional) church, was actually interdenominational. At one time I attended with her a meeting of the Judeo-Christian Society in my hometown, sitting among priests and rabbis, in an attempt to understand learned theological discourses. I didn't. At another time I chanced to be with her in a theater watching a modern play. I did not understand it either. Both encounters show the wide scope of the doctor's mind. The doctor was well versed in old and new literature. She was always probing the last, the essential questions of life, which are addressed by the church at large, Protestant and Catholic alike. In this sense, she walked with the wise. She shared what she read: "A soldier had served as a messenger in World War I. By his feet he saw a little flower and bent down. At that moment, a grenade exploded ahead and would have killed him had he further progressed." "Search for and never overlook the beautiful things in life," she advised. Or she told the short story of a man on his deathbed with wry humor. This man had called his son into his extensive library. "All these books are yours. Never loan any of them. They are all borrowed books."

We talked about death and dying. Sadly she had witnessed the mostly final, fatal outcome on a children's cancer ward. Would she consider living forever in the physical? "No way, not in this world. Going once through it suffices." Yes, we talked about heaven, too. How will it be? In other ways than we imagine, yet the same in some ways, a modern author said through an old, wise priest.

After our immigration, I corresponded with her, but then lost contact. I wished I had her new address in the city of Mannheim, but could not get it. Strangely, for years I thought of and prayed for her, although I was not even sure whether she was still alive. Yes, she was still alive. She thought of and prayed for me, too, but had suffered a debilitating stroke. The mystery was solved when I received a newspaper clipping from our hometown in 1981, containing the most complimentary obituary of the beloved doctor.

"Dr. Kaete Groh, a physician in Düsseldorf for more than fifty years, died at age ninety-three in Mannheim. Dr. Groh practiced medicine in the city center until her house was destroyed by bombs, and then in the suburb of Gerresheim for about thirty years. In 1972 she returned to her hometown of Mannheim, where she lived in a nursing home during the last five years after a stroke. Dr. Groh is well remembered by many citizens of Düsseldorf. She was a lady of special abilities, who served her suffering fellow citizens in accordance with her professional oath and her responsibility as a Christian. Many nights she stayed awake with lonely dying patients. Her fellow citizens' gratitude reaches far beyond her death."

Mine will last forever.

THE ENVIED CHESS PLAYER

"A heart at peace gives life to the body, but envy rots the bones."

—Proverbs 14:30

Among my parents' church friends were Mr. and Mrs. Hofmann. She was the gentlest lady I ever met, and he was a real fine gentleman who suffered from diabetes. In prior years he had owned and operated an excellent bakery, but then lost it through financial misjudgment. They had two daughters and one son, a friend of my older brothers. Willi was friendly. I remember him only with a genuine smile on his face. During the war, he served with the Panzers under Rommel in Africa. He told me that they used to fry eggs on these tanks in the hot continent. In due time, Willi became a prisoner of the Americans, was well treated and promptly released at the end of the war. He was not the only one who experienced good treatment. Just before I immigrated, I met a former German soldier who had spent time in our southern cotton fields, where he would have liked to stay. He really regretted that he could not accompany me to America and supported my sound decision.

After the war, I became senior Mr. Hofmann's frequent, always welcome visitor, since we both liked the game of chess. Whenever possible after school or during semester breaks, I spent time with him, played, and learned. Sometimes I won. By now he had lost both legs due to his affliction and sat with his stumps in a wheel chair. This gave me another fine reason to visit my elderly friend, combining a good deed with my own pleasure. There were times when I got him into a real fix. His whole body would react and shake because of the short cuts in his blood circulation. Then I always eased up on him.

Although his body was so sadly reduced, he remained effective and kept his family under gentle control. The Hofmanns lived now with their widowed daughter's family in walking distance from the chemical plant, where she and her brother Willi worked. The large company was family owned and practiced a capitalism without teeth, in other words with heart, since they cared about their employees in many ways, put not only bread and butter on their tables but provided also the Hofmann's modern apartment. This humanitarian attitude did not hinder the owners to grow their company into one of the most respected and profitable multinational enterprises during the past fifty years.

Mr. Hofmann Sr. was not an envious person. Strangely, he was envied, although not because of his masterly game of chess. Here are the circumstances. In the course of years, Willi had advanced from Panzers to Mercedes and become the chauffeur of one of the company big shots in marketing, a school friend of the owners. They drove all over Europe. On the weekend, Willi kept the Mercedes for personal and family use. As a good son, he would lift his father into a back seat by the window and drive him around to see nature or some urban beautification.

Now, in the old country streetcars would run in the middle of the street, and there were frequent stops. Willi had to stop then, too, and the people in the streetcar could take a real good look at the fortunate man on the back seat of the fancy Mercedes, being driven around by a chauffeur in a fine uniform. They looked down on my old friend and his hidden stumps with great envy. "If they only knew what a poor man I am, and in what wretched condition," he said to me without self-pity. Such are the illusions of the evil of envy. We imagine to be overlooked or underprivileged, while we are actually granted multiple favors, including personal mobility, health, and countless opportunities. The antidote is gratitude. There is only one way to live, namely positively in all circumstances, like Mr. Hofmann.

A CHANCE TO LEARN AND OBSERVE

"Let the wise listen and add to their learning, and let the discerning get guidance."

—*Proverbs 1:5*

My first school day was a day of celebration. At that time, learning was still considered an opportunity. My classmates and I celebrated this happy day in our schoolyard with a tall, decorated paper cone filled with candy. Every student got such a candy cone from his parents. I understand that this custom is still practiced in Germany today. This was a boys' school. Coed schools for boys and girls were not customary then and there. Public schools were even separated along the country's main confessional lines, evangelical or Catholic. I went to an "evangelical" elementary school and had my apprehensions. However, school went well with teacher Haase. We wrote on slate tablets for the first two years, then with ink in paper booklets.

The teacher liked his little fellows and let them do some acting in the classroom, e.g., the European version of the tortoise and the hare. The hare was fast, but never won the race because Mrs. Tortoise showed up ahead of time at the other end. We must have played well, because the teacher chose to present us to his daughter in a replay. However, our acting was then less persuading, since we started to reflect on our performance rather than being natural.

We read fairy tales, stories of 1001 nights, Robinson Crusoe. Occasionally we saw movies in school. One of them showed wood-laden sleighs in the Alps sliding downhill by gravity on logging roads. Little did I know that I would do something similar later, driving on snow-covered logging roads in the American boonies.

After two and a half years, the confessional separation of public schools was eliminated, and we had to change school to one much closer to home. The government, which did not think much of confessional groupings, ironically retained weekly instructions in religion for both Catholic and Protestant students. Another irony of that time, the nationalistic government did away with the German Sütterlin handwriting and printing and made Latin letters mandatory.

Our teacher at the new school was stern. He had lost one eye and part of his face in World War I. As a disciplinarian he used his bamboo rod frequently, and this daily routine was greatly respected. But he was also a good teacher.

My next stop, at age ten, was at a middle school that was a thirty-minute walk from home. Both my brothers had attended that school. Although it was public, it was not free. It cost my family ten marks per month and student. My parents deserve commendation that they sent five of their six children to middle schools despite bitter needs at home. My smart, oldest sister was excluded for financial reasons. I had to pass an entrance examination, and then landed in Gymnasium. Short, round, his head resembling a bowling ball, he taught German, history, and geography. Tall teacher Haake taught English. Both could be mean on occasion. Sandford was impatient, and Haake strongly minded our mispronunciations, particularly the "a" and "th" sounds. Stern and effective teacher Ochel taught English after 1941. For the first time, we felt a stiff wind blowing, which benefited me more than anything else. Little did I know that English should become my main language. My favorite subject, math, was taught well by teacher Baike.

The winter of 1941 to 1942 was extremely cold. Coal had to be saved, and schools were closed for several weeks. We were given lengthy home-work assignments. Since the bombing war progressed to the extent that it endangered everyone, the government started to send students away from home to country camps for their protection. But this idea did not appeal to me, and so I did not go immediately. Later I had the oppor-tunity to stay with relatives in a quaint city between the Harz and Huy Mountains. Never before had I seen such a beautiful city. Its middle school was located on a plaza near the gothic cathedral, and out of the window we looked far over the city to the Huy and its mountain top castle. Clouds sailed through blue, windy sky. The winds of change blew mightily. One could sense dramatic changes lying ahead.

I wish to share some local school experiences. When arrived in late August 1943, school had started already. I introduced myself as the new student, and the whole class laughed. They felt I was a funny person and accepted me. Mrs. Frischmeyer, my class teacher, lived with her custodi-an husband behind the cathedral in Gleim House, the residence of poet Gleim, one of Goethe's friends. She taught German, English, Geogra-phy, and History, sometimes combining the subjects. A large German map was raised, and she asked me to describe the fatherland in English. I did so very fluently for fifteen minutes. "Well", she said, "we are not yet that far advanced." Good teacher Ochel came through in me with his four seasons' charts describing so many colorful details. We were used to learning much vocabulary and then talked freely about the picture in front of us.

In history they were ahead. So I borrowed someone's notes and cop-ied them diligently, describing and sketching in colors the various battles of the Seven Year War (1756—1763) fought by Frederick the Great. But her teaching was not one-sided, as one might assume in wartime Ger-many. Mrs. Frischmeyer taught us American history, too, the fight for in-dependence, the meaning of the American flag, which I carefully copied in colors, as if a little love for America was already shining through my soul. My history notebook with the flag is still in my possession.

We entered the fateful year of 1944 with its invasion of the Normandy by Allied troops. A monthly English Reader was used to enhance our language skills. There, just a few weeks before the invasion on June 6, 1944, we would read in great objectivity about this pending event, its chances of success to overcome German Atlantic fortresses. I am still wondering how this English reader could have escaped the censors.

Mrs. Frischmeyer and I exchanged letters until she died after the war. She was a Christian of strong convictions. When I was still wavering, she reminded me of Hebrews 13:9,

"It is good to receive inner strength through God's grace."

The next teacher I wish to remember was Recktor Hoehnemann. He taught my favorite subjects, math and science. By teaching chemistry, when I was fourteen years old, he molded my future professional destiny. As teacher of an agricultural school, Hoehnenmann had published a book that he also used in our class. While sick and bored at home, I read his book and discovered neat chemical equations related among others to nitrate and phosphate fertilizers. The excitement about an orderly chemical world should never leave me. (At that time I did not yet learn about entropy.) Beyond that, the school in the quaint city was entertaining or amusing, since the challenges were moderate and some teachers provided a rather peaceful atmosphere.

Before I leave this school, I have to sketch three more teachers. There was no greater contrast than between the first two. One was our kind biology teacher, challenging in gentle ways, who showed us microbiological wonders in a drop of water under the microscope. The other one taught physical education. Actually, he seldom taught us, but set up a training schedule for gymnastics. He was sitting in a little office by the gym constantly doing paper work. Short, wiry, never smiling, an unpleasant fellow, he expected absolute submission even in personal matters. I was told that he did not survive the postwar years, when his life as a high party official was scrutinized by new authorities.

The third person was a kind math teacher. A few days before the Allied occupation in April, 1945, he saw me in a park near school, gave me a large pack of papers and asked me to bring them to a private house at eight in the evening. It was dark then. The door was cautiously opened. Inside was my kind teacher with others, one of whom reluctantly accepted the papers. I assume they were of some political nature. Evidently, a hot potato was passed at a discomforting time, while the clock ticked persistently into a new era toward the end of an unnecessary war.

LEARNING TO WORK

"If the ax is dull and its edge unsharpened, more strength is needed, but skill will bring success."

—Ecclesiastes 10:10

When school started again in the fall of 1945, we walked for forty-five minutes to one of the few suitable buildings left without major war damage. Classes were held in the afternoon, since another school used the building in the morning. We retained some teachers from the early war years, but got also new teachers, among them excellent English instructors. This was appropriate because of our location in the British occupation zone. The political climate was uncertain, since there were great social needs, including a starvation diet and housing shortage. Communists were loud in our hometown and were actually represented on the city council.

Dr. Deils, our French teacher, was a little, learned communist. He taught us the Marseillaise in French and never forgave me for my critical remarks about communism. Another authoritarian was Dr. Dapp, to whom fairness and student rights were foreign. All other teachers seemed to fit reasonably well into the new democratic era.

I was an enthusiastic science student and could not get enough of such stuff. So I attended evening courses provided by the newly created adult education system and also by a trade school. The satisfaction I received there was in stark contrast to our bitter living conditions. Because of a paper shortage, I wrote my notes on old calendars or on wrapping paper. In hindsight, this difficult period from 1945-1948 was also a most happy time in my life. There was so much hope, so much to do, and being so low, the only way out was up.

After graduation from middle school in 1947, I became a lab apprentice at a major chemical company [Henkel]. Everybody recognized that a school education is a necessary but insufficient requirement for work. Any work requires skills and training. The European apprentice system has been an excellent and practical way to address this need. It involves the commitment of employers and apprentices, including their willingness to work for little. Unfortunately, the idea hardly took hold in America, which probably contributed to the problems of our youth with lack of purpose and motivation. On the other hand, we have BOCES[22] and college courses directed toward practical, tangible goals, for instance in nursing and in engineering work student programs. While such opportunities are not lacking, formal and wide-spread work training is missing in this country. It is also interesting to note that West Germany's so-called economic miracle in the 1950's benefited from the abundance of skilled labor at a time of great demand in a newly created free market economy. Only a spark was needed to set it into motion, i.e., a kick-start by the Marshall Plan.

My employer provided an exemplary apprentice program, including rotations through various labs, problem solving sessions every morning from seven to seven-thirty, except for Saturdays, when we had sports from seven to nine. Once a week, we went to an occupational school. For three months, every apprentice (including office clerks) had to make metal objects, working with files on vises to meet required dimensions. Ever since, I have much respect for people who make a living using such practical skills and intelligence.

---

22. Boards of Cooperative Educational Services

Since I desired to get a high school diploma, I took private Latin lessons. In 1948, I enrolled in the city's evening high school. My schedule was as follows: Get up at 5:30 in the morning, walk fifteen minutes to catch a streetcar by 6:30, work in the lab from 7 AM to 4 PM, take the streetcar to the old city center, learn and study from 5 to 8 PM, take another streetcar home, do homework till 11 PM, and start the cycle again at 5:30 in the morning. On Saturdays, we worked till 1 PM and had school from 2 to 5 PM. On some Sundays, I was wondering why I was pushing myself so hard, while my friends began to enjoy nature walks and other nice things of life, which slowly emerged after 1948. Now I know why and have no regrets. Persistence pays. In the fall of 1950, I graduated from evening high school and also passed all my tests at the Chamber of Commerce as a lab technician. Free at last. The company rewarded me then with a modest scholarship for one year to study chemistry, then kindly renewed it yearly, eight times.

In the fall of 1950, I became a student at the University of Cologne and listened to professor Alder, a Nobel Prize winner in organic chemistry, who lectured in a somewhat repaired ruin. I commuted from home, but was really only a part-time student, since housing in Cologne was non-existent. Neither was a place in the lab. Without it, chemistry would become a never-ending field of study. Therefore, I tried to get into Bonn, and succeeded in the spring of 1951. I still see myself walking across the large plaza near the railroad station, asking a senior citizen where I could find housing. He directed me to a big concrete air-raid bunker which was subdivided into small cells and populated by a colony of university students, who praised the bunker's quietness, electric light, and ventilation. The place was near the Chemical Institute, made famous by first Nobel Prize winner Kekule from the turn of the century. His likeness in front of the building was flanked by two bronze lions, which were scrubbed weekly in his honor during prewar times. Well, I did not spend any time in the bunker, but several years in Kekule's holy halls. My housing was with Mrs. Brown in Godesberg, who lived in a crowded old city street. The room was tiny. So were my rent ($6.25/month) and grocery bill (less than $20 per month), since I lived off only four staples, i.e., rye bread, sugar, margarine, and buttermilk. She was very kind, provided cookies at Christmas time and protected her dog with a coat bearing his name, Fiffy. Mrs. Brown would have loved to protect her husband, too, an unemployed policeman. He could not adjust to the harsh, unfriendly postwar reality, smoked and drank himself to death. I still see him and other desperados vainly smiling in a Godesberg bar, where I went to look for him on her behalf.

The bicycle was my means of transportation, usually on the main highway, occasionally also along the scenic Rhine River, with a view on the Seven Mountains. I lived with Mrs. Brown for three semesters, exploring by bike the Eifel and Hunsrueck Mountains and surrounding castles. For many hours, I relaxed and studied on the scenic cemetery by the Godesburg. A literal translation of such place means peace court. The quiet setting suited my studies in summer and provided peace during at time of adjustment to a strange and challenging school environment.

The university had excellent, enthusiastic chemistry professors and a great tradition. One professor shared an interesting story from his student years, when he was advised to get out of chemistry. His successful life and career would have been quite different if he had given up. I attended several memorial lectures and others at the occasion of honorable degrees. There were difficulties, challenges, and successes. I passed my first degree with honors, and expediently worked on my second degree by taking care of mandatory lab courses during semester breaks. My friend Wolfgang and I prepared ourselves well for these major examinations, and we passed with flying colors. We met every other day in my room in a village north of the city, then studied alone for one day, and alternately served as our own examiners, while feasting on tomato salad prepared with onions, pepper, salt, and olive oil. His profound understanding of physical chemistry led to his later call as professor and major contributor in the field of polagraphy. Still young, he was to die of a heart attack while on the way to a meeting in Toronto. I tried to contact him from Japan and then received the sad news in America like a faint echo of his family's grief. Carpe Diem! Our days are numbered, whether we are granted few or many.

I wanted to do my thesis with a professor who had just received a call to Munich. When I joined him there, I found some free time before the semester started, and so I took my bike into the Alps for a long weekend, all the way to Tirol. My first Munich residence was in Schwabing, where I occupied a tiny room (for $11/Month) ten bike minutes from school. After three semesters I moved to Grosshadern, and for the last semester to Kreuz Street, across from a 500 year-old church. My student years in Munich, where I served as a lab instructor, were fulfilling. The city and surroundings were inspiring. After our marriage, Magdalena and I lived for a while in Grosshadern. She worked for a publishing house in Munich, and later typed my thesis. I received my final degree in time to return home two days before Christmas. My suitcase was loaded with books and fixed the taxi driver to the ground when he tried to lift it into the trunk of his Mercedes. He made me promise not to study over Christmas, which I gladly granted after so many years of fun, excitement, but also frustration over a seemingly never ending student career. But "everything has an end," my father used to say, "only a sausage has two ends."

PROTECTED

"Others went out on the sea in ships. They saw the works of the Lord, His wonderful deeds in the deep. For He spoke and stirred up a tempest that lifted high the waves. They mounted up to the heavens and went down to the depths. In their peril their courage melted away. Then they cried out to the Lord in their trouble. He stilled the storm to a whisper; the waves of the sea were hushed. Let them give thanks to the Lord for His unfailing love."

—From Psalm 107:23-31

Surrounded by dangers, we are usually not thinking that they may affect us personally. They may appear suddenly as accidents and crimes, or emerge slowly as changing living conditions, war, or illness. Our work environment, too, is potentially hazardous. That's why ever improving safety precautions and training are put in to place. The chemical profession is not the most dangerous occupation, but it has its share of tragedies and avoidable mishaps. It may expose the human body to a variety of special dangers, i.e., poisons, slowly acting harmful agents, quickly harming gases and liquids, fires, or explosions.

I remember a man who burnt to death, have met people who lost an eye or limb, one with a crippled finger due to a freak accident, and one who lost his total eyesight in an unpredictable explosion of a few milligrams of a solid he tried to analyze. This happened to be the last experiment for his doctoral thesis.

Generally working safely with harmful substances, I received at one time a small dosage of gases that seemed to penetrate my brain, and I experienced and extinguished numerous laboratory fires. Only once was I involved in an explosion that could have killed me and others. It was not even chemical, but physical in nature. I might not have been responsible then because of my apprentice status, but I certainly was the instrumental factor. We developed a water-soluble form of cellulose for use as wallpaper glue. For this purpose, a calculated amount of methyl chloride had to be transferred into an autoclave. This gas, liquefied at 24.5° C, was collected in a small steel bomb. By warming the steel bomb in hot water later, the chemical was then transferred into the autoclave. It was at this stage that I left the lab to get distilled water elsewhere in the building. When I came back, I noticed that an explosion had occurred. Evidently by enormous liquid pressure, the steel bomb with a thickness of about one quarter of an inch had ruptured from its bottom to the valve. This sent it up to the concrete ceiling like a rocket, swinging the attached copper capillary like a whip that smashed several glass flasks on a top shelf. Deflected by a concrete beam, the ruptured bomb descended then into the middle of the lab between four chemists and engineers in close proximity. No one was hurt, and I had left in the nick of time. As I recall these circumstances, I cannot help but see the guarding force of providence steering the course of events. More often than we realize does God protect us from harm. Why does it happen elsewhere? We don't have the answer. Most things conceivable are also possible. Thankfulness is our appropriate response for being spared.

PREMATURE MOURNING

"Look, there on the mountains, the feet of one who brings good news."

Nahum 1:15

As a teenager I got acquainted with Huckleberry Finn when I read Mark Twain in German. Since then I learned that the author possessed also musical talent, which he demonstrated when their house was flooded by the Mississippi. As his Dad floated downstream in his bed, Mark accompanied him on the piano. The Mississippi is my favorite American river. We have travelled for hundreds of miles along its banks and actually waded through the Mississippi at its humble beginnings, where it emerges as a clear creek out of Lake Itasca in northern Minnesota. The source is so much north that one should assume a final discharge into the Arctic Ocean, like the Red River's discharge via a series of Canadian lakes. Its source is far to the southwest of Lake Itasca. But a mountain range, not shown on most maps, blocks a northern course of the Mississippi, so that it meanders toward the east, south, west, and south again, until it assumes its purpose as America's main artery. The historic Hudson is second in my appreciation, the Ohio third with its Indian and early American folklore, while the Missouri is too erosive for my taste.

One can establish a friendly relationship with a river as with a person, and if separated for a while, one desires to renew the friendship. So it is also with my favorite European river, the Rhine, not far from whose banks I was born. This river was praised in song and rhyme by Heinrich Heine (1797-1856), the famous poet of my hometown, who wrote "Loreley" named after a rock and legend in the most scenic Rhine valley. Heine died poor in Paris, after he had talked not so kindly about the Prussians, who in turn did not think too kindly of him. Yet he became known throughout the world, as I found out in Japan where friends remembered him and recited "Loreley."

The Rhine is about one thousand feet wide at my hometown and busily carries freight in international traffic. Shared by four countries (Switzerland, France, Germany, and Holland), their barges would transport commodity items such as coal and chemicals. Kilometer numbers and subdivisions clearly marked the positions on the river. Powerful boats slowly pulled up to six heavy barges on steel cables. Deeply immersed, only a foot or two would rise above water. As teenage boys we were daring swimmers and used these barges for joy rides upstream. I started this practice at age thirteen. First I identified one of the barges as my target, then factored in the downstream drift by the current and swam perpendicular to the river's bank. Somewhere in the middle of the barge I would hold on to its upper rim. I noticed at this time a fair speed of the barge relative to the current, even though one could almost keep pace with it by walking at the bank. It took a firm grip onto the barge's rim, because it was riveted and your fingers would hurt if you would allow them to slide over these rivets. The current would then sweep your body downstream and up, helping your legs to climb onto the barge. This was a proven method to convert yourself from swimmer to passenger. The skippers were not thrilled and sometimes chased us, but more often resigned themselves to having us on board. After a kilometer or so, I would go to the ten-foot high bow, where the barge created a mighty wave, dove into it and swam back to my point of origin.

On one hot Sunday afternoon, I left my sister at the bank and swam toward my chosen barge on the far side of the river. Because of the distance, I miscalculated and missed it, as one would miss a train at the station. Being so far on the other side, I swam to where I could stand in the water and waited for the next train of barges to appear, which took about fifteen minutes. I picked a barge, climbed onto it and found it full of travelers in their swimming trunks. None made an effort to swim back, so that I think now they went officially on board somewhere downstream for a lengthy excursion. I did not want to leave earlier than they did particularly since I knew two of these people. Thus my journey took me far beyond the normal duration of a joy ride. When I finally jumped overboard and swam back to my sister, I might have been away perhaps two hours. There she sat crying and mourning my death by drowning, and how would she tell our mother, who had already lost two sons, and I was the only one remaining? When Mark Twain was a senior citizen, some newspaper announced his death prematurely, and he replied in style that this announcement was vastly exaggerated. He was then both famous and old enough for the press to anticipate his passing. I had none of these attributes, and only a terse statement might have been printed that another dumb boy had nothing better to do but to drown during summer. But, as I stated, the river was my friend, and it carried me safely like a cork to my destination. However, I received a slight punishment on the way back by having my leg rubbed bloody on a submerged steel cable. Beyond that, I found assurance that my sister loved me and certainly would have remembered me for a long time.

SOLID FRIENDSHIP BUILT ON WATER

"There is a friend who sticks closer than a brother."

—Proverbs 18:24

The quaint city was surrounded by great scenery, with mountains as well as water to enjoy. A small river flowed through fields, forests and an old village. There we kept our paddleboat. Actually, it belonged to my friend Karl Heinz. We always rode our bikes to that village, and then the boat on the rocky, sometimes shallow, secluded river. Here we spent some of the happiest, most peaceful hours of our lives, while a grim and unforgiving war continued elsewhere. It must have been the war's last autumn time when we paddled on the quiet river and surprisingly met someone on the banks in front of a small cabin, the first time we met anyone in the river's vicinity. The young man pretended to be a soldier on leave, but I believe now that he was a deserter. He was quite scared. Later he accompanied us by bike into town. I am not in favor of deserters, but I hope this man survived and escaped the futility of those days.

Our boyhood friendship of only eighteen months has continued for a lifetime under unusual circumstances. Karl Heinz and I parted our ways in 1945, when the Iron Curtain descended and physically separated us. For the next forty-eight years, including the tension filled Cold War era, we corresponded and sometimes exchanged tokens of friendship. We both concluded university studies, married, raised three children, became active church members, deplored the existence of totalitarianism, and thought on the same wavelength. These similarities stand in stark contrast with the societies in which we lived, freedom in the West versus communism in the East, with all its ugly forms of oppression, economical short falls, and spying. About two percent of the East German population spied on their fellow men. Our correspondence had to be guarded because of the communist censorship. They would read his letters as well as mine. But occasionally some opportunities allowed Karl Heinz to express himself freely, and I knew how he felt, which in turn let me encourage him and relay the message that he was not forgotten. Picture postcards from my travels in Europe, North America, and Japan opened a window to the world that he was not permitted to see with his own eyes.

Then a miracle of God happened, as he put it. The Berlin Wall and communism collapsed, people were freed, and the church took a sigh of relief. This opened the gate for a grand reunion, our golden anniversary of friendship, which we planned and celebrated well in the Land of the Free. Karl Heinz and his wife Johanna came to America as our guests. It was the longest trip they ever took, and the most rewarding time for all of us. There was so much to tell, so much to share, some bottled-up tension relieved of injustice they had endured. Our friendship had outlasted the Berlin Wall, the Iron Curtain, and communism, and proved to be a manifestation of hope and faith.

OF GOOD POWERS

For the kingdom of God is not a matter of talk but of power.

I Corinthians 4:20

You may know His incomparable great power for us who believe.

Ephesians 1:19

It is good to hear of them early in life. Better yet, to long and search for them. But best, is a direct affiliation with those good powers through life and death.

As a three-year old recipient of bedside stories, I learned of a small shepherd boy who was empowered to slay the arrogant Goliath. Then I heard of other mysterious biblical stories. Were they still relevant? At fourteen, when I helped a senior citizen pull his cart, I received unsolicited and unexpected advice. "Anything that may happen to me, has to pass God first," said the old man, whom I met only that one time. To him those powers were relevant. This got my attention. He must have been under a heavy burden, but he was not alone. Perhaps those good powers even sent me to help him. I watched then people and events, and it became clear that they were moved by unseen realities. How did people respond to circumstances? It was not written on their faces. Why did certain events happen? Evidently, there was no rational answer or predictability in many cases. Yet, powerful events did happen, and people responded to them in remarkable ways.

The same tragic event could make or break a person. My mother's school friend in northern Germany and her dentist husband lost their only son in the war. The poor woman would still grieve after twenty years, so that my dear mother consoled her by letter and by visiting. Where did she take the power from, she who had lost her eyesight, two sons, her husband and a daughter? There was Mrs. Schwechten in Munich, the widow of a consul in colonial Africa during World War I, interned with others and mistreated. "Only those with faith would live on," she remarked. Is faith itself a real power? Or is it a tool to tap the great pool of those mysterious good powers? Who could protect or guide us when we are at our wits end? As we look back, we detect a series of **solid steps in shifting sand**, which have become the basis of our short stories on a long trail of tests.

I feel inadequate to write about the good powers in our lives. What I can say is neither profound nor theological, just the confirmation that there have been powers in our lives, and these powers have been good. Further it is in order to use the plural form. God appears in three persons, Father, Son, and Holy Spirit, and we hear about a multitude of heavenly hosts. Awe and respect are appropriate. Obviously we have no monopoly. Hundreds of generations and contemporaries have experienced these good powers, which have lightened their paths and their burdens. These powers are effective and real, yet their definition and description are beyond our comprehension. Hidden realities are driving people to their deeds, but they are not accessible by an outside observer. They are not limited to the rational world either, but are deeply embedded in self with its many irrational manifestations. You look for reality as the sole criterion? Here we are dealing with ultimate reality. Pastor Ted Hegre helped my understanding when he described in a model the human spirit embedded in the Holy Spirit like a shell. Our inner self, even our lives may be surrounded by good powers in most trying circumstances. The final outcome, however, is not necessarily a "happy ending." As Corrie Ten Boom stated, "The worst may happen, but the best remains." These good powers imply a definite choice of orientation and final destination. You are looking for people where these good powers have become most visible? They are few. Someone said, "Saints are people who make it easier for us to believe." Yet such people have lived in this terrible century too, and their loyalty has been most exclusively focused on God. No one else has persuaded me more of the reality of these powers and their goodness than the man I describe below, although I never met him in person.

He was born into a large, happy family of achievers and grew up with a natural desire to help others. Early on he displayed energy, concentration, objectivity, clarity, simplicity, tact, and humility; an athletic, blond giant. He shunned empty phrases and excessive emotions. A brilliant student of theology, he was recognized as a doctor of divinity at age twenty-one, then served as vicar in Barcelona, Spain. At twenty-three, he taught theology in Berlin University. Three years later, the National Socialists came to power. Within four weeks he went on the air and warned the people against their idol and misleader. Two years after this example of his clear discernment and his return from a pastorate in London, he was forbidden to preach or speak in Berlin, or to enter the city. He then conducted an illegal seminary for the Confessing Church on the coast of the Baltic Sea. The Confessing Church was an organized opposition group within the Evangelical Church in Germany. In 1939, he visited for the second time his friends at the Union Theological Seminary in New York. Reinhold Niebuhr described him as an "exceptionally gifted and theologically educated young man." Then the war broke out in Europe. Against the urgings of his American friends, he chose to return to Germany. "I would have no right to participate rebuilding Christian life in Germany after the war, if I would not share their trials. Christians in Germany will face the terrible decision, either to wish defeat of their nation so that Christianity may survive, or to wish victory and then destroy our civilization. I know which of these possibilities to choose, but I cannot make this decision and remain safe myself." Thus he chose to stand out against the politically organized evil of those days. "The task is not to look after the victims of a mad man, who drives a car into a crowd, but to do everything to stop his driving." Consequently, he participated in the German resistance. He was forbidden to teach and publish, but he wrote several books, most of them published posthumously. That's how I made his acquaintance. At thirty-seven, he was imprisoned; at thirty-eight, put into a concentration camp; at thirty-nine, executed just days before Flossenbürg was liberated by American troops. He was Dietrich Bonhoeffer. His family lost also his uncle, his brother, two brothers-in-law, and a close family friend who all stood up against evil.

A few years ago, I met in a German church eighty-year old Mrs. Rosen. She and her husband were present when Pastor Niemoeller was arrested in Berlin and sent to Dachau concentration camp in 1937. They were among Bonheoffer's friends. I asked what kind of person Bonhoeffer was. "He was very bright and very musical, and was very soft." She used the German word "weich," but probably meant soft-hearted, compassionate, and she shared with me recently published pictures of Bonhoeffer's life, martyr and hero in this terrible century. An example persuades more than a thousand sermons. Are good powers defeated in this world? They remain most real, although the individual person may be torn by evil. As stated before, "the worst may happen, but the best remains." At New Year 1945, Bonhoeffer's parents received a poem from their son, which reflects best the nature of those good powers.

OF GOOD POWERS

By D. Bonhoeffer (Translation)

Faithfully and quietly covered by good powers,
Wonderfully protected and comforted,
That's the way I want to live these days,
And want to go with you into a New Year.

The old year still tries to torture our hearts.
The difficult burden of evil days still oppresses us.
O LORD, give our intimidated souls the salvation
For which you prepared us.

If you should present to us the difficult, bitter
Cup of suffering, filled to the upper rim,
We will gratefully take it, without trembling,
Out of your good and loving hand.

But if you want to give us joy once more
Of this world and its sun's brightness,
Then we'll think about the past,
Then our life will belong to you completely.

Today warmly and quietly, let the candles burn,
That you brought into our darkness.
Lead us together again, if possible.
We know that your light shines in the night.

Now as serenity entirely covers us,
Let us hear the full melody of your kingdom,
Which invisibly surrounds us,
The high song of praise of all your children.

Wonderfully sheltered by good powers,
We expect with confidence whatever may come.
GOD is with us in the evening and in the morning,
And quite certainly on every new day.

PHOTOGRAPHS

BACKGROUND ECHOES

THE SERVANT OF THE SICK

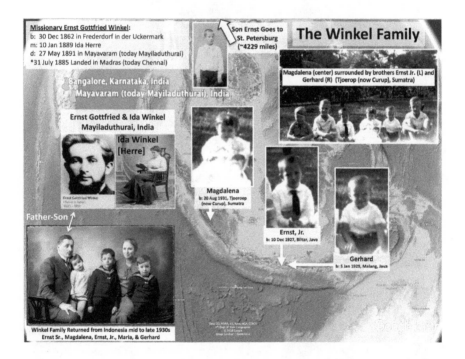

Missionary Ernst Gottfried Winkel:
b: 30 Dec 1862 in Frederdorf in der Uckermark
m: 10 Jan 1889 Ida Herre
d: 27 May 1891 in Mayavaram (today Mayiladuthurai)
*31 July 1885 Landed in Madras (today Chennai)

Son Ernst Goes to St. Petersburg (~4229 miles)

The Winkel Family

Bangalore, Karnataka, India
Mayavaram (today Mayiladuthurai), India

Magdalena (center) surrounded by brothers Ernst Jr. (L) and Gerhard (R) (Tjoerop (now Curup), Sumatra)

Ernst Gottfried & Ida Winkel
Mayiladuthurai, India

Ida Winkel [Herre]

Ernst Gottfried Winkel

Magdalena
b: 20 Aug 1931, Tjoeroep (now Curup), Sumatra

Ernst, Jr.
b: 10 Dec 1927, Blitar, Java

Gerhard
b: 5 Jan 1929, Malang, Java

Father-Son

Winkel Family Returned from Indonesia mid to late 1930s
Ernst Sr., Magdalena, Ernst, Jr., Maria, & Gerhard

EARLY VISION WARNS

Mid to late 1890s
Ernst ("Erny") Winkel in St. Petersburg
Son of Missionary Ernst Gottfried Winkel who died of cholera May 27, 1891

1930s & 1990
Ernst, Magdalena, and Gerhard Winkel on Grüenhof Farm, Pomerania
and visiting in 1990 with Mike once the Berlin Wall came down

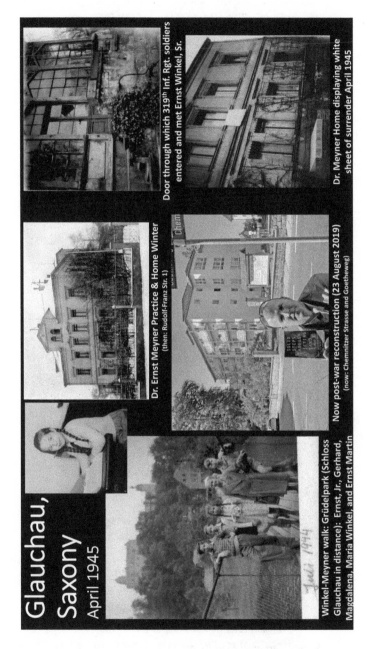

Glauchau, Saxony
April 1945

Door through which 319th Inf. Rgt. soldiers entered and met Ernst Winkel, Sr.

Dr. Meyner Home displaying white sheet of surrender April 1945

Dr. Ernst Meyner Practice & Home Winter (then: Rudolf-Franz Str. 1)

Now post-war reconstruction (23 August 2019) (now: Chemnitzer Strasse and Goetheweg)

Winkel-Meyner walk: Grüdelpark (Schloss Glauchau in distance): Ernst, Jr., Gerhard, Magdalena, Maria Winkel, and Ernst Martin

1944–1945
Glauchau, Germany

THE THANKFUL SOWER

1935
Thomas Klose during his last year

Grave of Thomas Klose & Marie Klose [Goral].
Discovered 24 August 2019 in the mostly destroyed Protestant Cemetery in
Ottosberg, Dutchy of Posen [today Korpysy, Poland]
Thomas Klose (b: 21.12.1851; d: 1.9.1935)
Marie [Marianne] Klose [Goral] (b: 11.2.1852; d: 9.1.1931)
-1 Thessalonians 4:16

GOLDEN YEARS END

1903–1905 and 1914–1918, Adolf Gustav Rauhut
Pre-war with the 7. West Prussian Infantry Regiment Nr. 155 (Left-standing left) and
64th Reserve Infantry Regiment (Right-seated with dog)

Master of the Field Kitchen (standing above others)

1917, Adolf Gustav Rauhut (Right)
Iron Cross Recipient

MIDFIELD TESTS

THE CHICKADEES

Adolf Gustav Rauhut in 1913
Düsseldorf Streetcar Operator (Standing on Car 232)

1931, Horst Rauhut

WHEN WHITSUNDAY TURNED RED

1930s Interwar Period
Henkel Fireman (6th from Left)

HOUSE ASSOCIATION

1930s–1940s
Horst Rauhut Birth Home, Ruhrtalstraße 6, Düsseldorf, Germany

GARDEN MEMORIES & ON WHEELS

1933 & 1951
Horst on his bike at the family "Schreber Garten" and exploring after the war

A LADY OF FAITH

1938, Rauhut Family
Johanna, Horst, , Adolf Sr., Klara (Sitting) Maria, Adolf Jr., Helmut, Hilde (Standing)

1965 in Rockville, Maryland
Johanna Rauhut [Klose] "A Lady of Faith"
12 August 1887 to 22 December 1972

AUNT BELA'S FARM

1936, Andreas Johann Rauhut Farm
Johanna Rauhut [Klose], Andreas Johann Rauhut, Adolf Rauhut Jr., Karoline Rauhut
[Jaensch], Kaltenborn near Ulrikenfeld (west of Grabow nad Prosna, Poland)

1938 and 2019, Andreas Johann Rauhut Grave in Ulrikenfeld
"March 15, 1855 to April 6, 1938. Loved-Wept for-Not Forgotten. Rest in peace."
[Vicinity Kaliszkowice Kaliskie, Poland; 24 August 2019]

OUT OF THE BLUE SKY

1930s–2000s, Halberstadt, Germany

SOLID FRIENDSHIP BUILT ON WATER

Reunion of Halberstadt friends Karl Heinz and Horst
Johanna and Karl Heinz Philipp, Magdalena and Horst, and Monika, Ken, and Heidi
Harris

A CHANCE TO LEARN AND OBSERVE

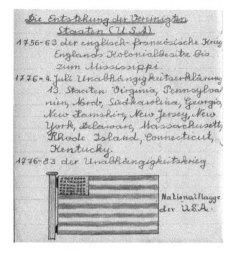

1943, Dad's history notebook from Mrs. Frischmeyer's class

LEARNING TO WORK

Horst Rauhut celebrates achieving his PhD with colleagues

OUTBACK TALES

FULL LIFE BEGINS

16 July 1957, Wedding Day, Rauhut-Winkel Family Members and Friends

1967 and 1969. The Young Rauhut Family

1973, The Rauhut Family enjoying Allegany State Park

2006, Rauhut–Harris–Wingard Family (Willow Road, Cuba, NY)

IMMIGRANTS

1956, Zimmermann Family in Winnipeg
Hans and Maria Anna [Rauhut] with children Waltraud next to Helmut, Ingrid (right),
Klaus (back), and youngest Hanna

1964, The Rauhut Family days before emigrating to the U.S.A.

18 June 1988 & 3 Oct 1990
Berlin Wall (from a friend's home) & Brandenburg Gate (Reunification Day)

3 October 1990, Brandenburg Gate
First sunset on a reunified Germany

FROM HOTEL MARYLAND TO MANITOBA

1965, Dad, Kay and Sigi Metzger, Ernst Winkel
Berens River, Manitoba, Canada

CHURCH IN AMERICA

1975, Haskell Community Church

SILENT NIGHT CHRISTMAS REFLECTIONS

Christmas 1936, Magdalena (seated right, 5 years old) with the Meyner Family in Glauchau, Germany

Christmas 1965, With Winkel parents in Rockville, Maryland

BEST FRIENDS

Horst hiking with best friends Fluffy & Samson

TYME AND TYDE

February 1952, Ernst Brockhaus, wife Emmi, son Helmut and Dad on a hike

August 1951, Ernst and Emmi Brockhaus and Dad on a hike

28 May 1987, Horst visiting his old friend

ANOTHER NOTABLE LADY OF FAITH

*3 October 1990, Magdalena Rauhut [Winkel]
with Kaiser Wilhelm Memorial Church in background Berlin, Germany*

2004, Hannah and Jacob welcome Daddy home from Tikrit, Iraq

FELLOW WORKERS

1964-1970

Dr. Horst W. Rauhut, Department of the Army (last on right)

Successfully attained 3 U.S. Patents while at Harry Diamond Laboratories

United States Patent Office

3,515,612

Patented June 2, 1970

1

3,515,612
METHOD OF MAKING FOAM SANDWICH
Horst W. Rauhut, Rockville, Md., assignor to the United
States of America as represented by the Secretary of
the Army
Filed Mar. 24, 1967, Ser. No. 626,368
Int. Cl. B32b 3/26, 27/40, 5/18
U.S. Cl. 156—79   4 Claims

ABSTRACT OF THE DISCLOSURE

A low dielectric loss foam sandwich structure useful in
delay lines made by coating two substrate sheets with a
resinous mixture containing 10–70 parts of an ethylene-
propylene terpolymer, 30–90 parts of a styrene monomer
or an inert volatile solvent, 1–2 parts of a free radical
polymerization initiator and 1–5 parts of a blowing agent;
heating the coated substrate sheets at 60–80° C. to foam
the resinous mixture; placing the resultant foamed sur-
faces face to face in the form of a sandwich; and heating
the sandwich at 70–90° C. to complete polymerization
and vulcanization of the foamed resinous mixture.

2

FIG. 3 is a similar view wherein two of the foam
coated substrates shown in FIG. 2 are being placed foam
face to foam face to form a sandwich structure; and

FIG. 4 is a view similar to that of FIG. 3 after the
foamed resin core of the sandwich structure has been
cured.

The ethylene-propylene terpolymer employed in the
foam sandwich of my invention may be any conventional
unvulcanized ethylene-propylene terpolymer. Such terpolymers usually contain about 35–66 mole percent of
ethylene, about 34–55 mole percent of propylene and
about 1–10% by weight of a non-conjugated diene such
as 5-methylene-2-norbornene, dicyclopentadiene, 1,4-
hexadiene and the like. Terpolymers of this type are con-
ventionally vulcanized at temperatures between 130–180°
C. and up to 205° C.

Since styrene itself is relatively slow curing, a faster
curing styrene-type system containing styrene and/or one
or more more reactive substituted styrenes such as di-
chlorostyrene, divinylbenzene and the like may be employed in the present process in order to accelerate the
curing reaction. The term styrene monomer as used herein refers to styrene, substituted styrenes and/or mixtures
thereof.

4. OUTBACK TALES
1964 – 2000

SHORT TALES, MOSTLY FROM AMERICA,

WHICH CONFIRMED IN NUMEROUS

CIRCUMSTANCES THAT GOD IS GOOD

AND SHOULD BE TRUSTED

FULL LIFE BEGINS

"A wife of noble character is her husband's crown."

—*Proverbs 12:4*

"She is worth far more than rubies. Her husband has full confidence in her and lacks nothing of value."

—*Proverbs 31:10-11*

We met first in church and youth group. Her brothers were my good friends. Not until her twentieth birthday did I show obvious interest in Magdalena, when I gave her a ceramic gift. Since it came from me, she sensed I must be serious. We began to date, and dated for three years, got engaged, and then waited for another three years before we got married because I wanted to complete my studies first and have a "basis for existence." This long waiting had precedents as long ago as the mid 1800's, when the "basis for existence" did often not materialize until people were well into their thirties. How times have changed.

Magdalena has been a strong and positive influence in my life ever since. There were those long hikes, when she listened to my enthusiastic tales of chemistry, of which it seemed she never could get enough. There were numerous letters and telephone calls. There was frustration about being separated. When we married, we went first to a state office as required. Later we celebrated a Christian service in her parent's large apartment, and then enjoyed our wedding dinner. Photographs of the party show a happy group of relations and friends. Late afternoon we left for the Lüneburg Heath on our honeymoon. We stayed there about two weeks, then concluded our trip at Hamburg and Blankenese on the Elbe river. Had I been a Hamburger, I would have been a "Shyburger." I did not want people to sense we were on our honeymoon. Now, after several decades of a good marriage, I have significantly changed and even hold hands in public.

While I waited for the wedding, two events and visions occurred within a few days. Uncle Martin [Metzker] was severely sick and one feared he might die. He was our favorite, the artist of our paintings. On several visits, I had brought him self-made "Kuemmel" (caraway) drink, influenced by my involvement with chemistry. One time, during a serious episode of "Gone With The Wind," the stopper popped in the movie theater, but luckily landed in Magdalena's lap. People said "Prost!" because they thought we were taking a comforter.

Well, two weeks before our wedding, as I rode my bike in Munich, a hearse pulled up before me, and I sensed his [Uncle Martin's] death and wondered about our wedding. Then a marriage coach pulled up, and I sensed our approaching wedding despite death in the family. And that's the way it happened in short order. In fact, he had said to Aunt Mimi to go ahead with the wedding in any case. Of course, she was then somewhat quiet.

We lived in a large room of the Winkel apartment, while I worked as a summer student. But my instructor job at the university required my departure in October. So we were separated until Christmas. In January, we could both move into my nice room in Grosshadern. Magdalena started to work with a publishing house until August of that year. I have never regretted our courtship and marriage. It was one of the very good things the Lord sent our way, which can't be rationalized or fully explained. A good decision was followed by a life-long commitment, care, and love.

The first year passed quickly, and after my last exam shortly before Christmas, I returned to our hometown. Right after New Year I began my career as an industry chemist, and in June our first daughter [Birgit] was born. I was away on business but returned in time for her birth. She was quite beautiful and much attached to her Dad. From my USA / Canada trip two years later, she received and warmly accepted a large, stuffed, Canadian dog. When our second daughter [Monika] was born almost three years later, she extended her love to her baby sister immediately. Magdalena did not easily recover, and within three months became seriously ill. The doctor recommended a diet home in the Eifel Mountains to recuperate, and we went there in April when violets and wild cherries started to bloom. Waerland was a Swedish dietitian and promoter of healthy vegetarian food, particularly of raw vegetables and "long milk" (a Swedish yogurt variety which drew long strings). The children stayed with friends during that time.

One week, Magdalena became quite concerned about the baby. We found out that she was in the city clinic with a serious digestive disorder. I drove there immediately and saw our tiny daughter looking in peace like a shining angel on the arms of her nurse, so fragile that light and air appeared to go right through her little body. The sight filled my heart with great compassion. When we prayed for her recovery, the good Lord heard our prayers, and also those for Magdalena's health.

With these two girls we immigrated to America in 1964, which will be the subject of another story. Before Christmas 1965, Magdalena had a miscarriage. In her weak condition, we went to Constitution Hall, where Handel's Hallelujah was sung by the Greater Washington choir. This musical and Christian experience provided great inspiration and comfort. One year later in December, our son [Mike] was born in Washington, D.C. We were then group health members with an excellent insurance plan. This gave me the idea that everything was paid. But when I picked him up, the charge was still fifty dollars. Yet I had only twenty dollars with me, which I used as a down payment.[23] Then I promptly paid him off within the next three months. He was adored by his sisters in the house in Maryland, at this small and comfortable, sunny home, where we all lived happily.

---

23. Dad loved to share this "installment plan" story and even did so with me two weeks before his passing.

IMMIGRANTS

"Where you go I will go, and where you stay I will stay. Your people will be my people, and your God my God."

—*Ruth 1:16*

Every story has its background; immigration is no exception. I had no intent to leave Germany when my oldest sister's family left for Canada in late autumn of 1955. But the experience preconditioned me. I still did not have such inclinations as an industry chemist in 1960. When my employer sent me to America in early 1961, I traveled also to Winnipeg, and wondered about my destiny. The North American continent fascinated me: the large, empty airfield in Baltimore, a relaxed man walking through sunshine and snow, the old hotel with its prewar elevator, the colonial atmosphere and simplicity in a business associate's home, a large state park on Lake Erie, the mighty falls of the Niagara River, the train ride to Chicago, Minneapolis, and Canada; vastness, scenery, and people who were driving rather than being driven. Ice fishing on the Mississippi near LaCrosse, arctic reminders in North Dakota, Manitoba Junction (where a small train took me into Canada); my sister's new home, and Lower Fort Garry on the Red River of the North. On March 6, the ice on Falcon Lake in western Ontario was still three feet thick, as shown by fishing holes and by cars parked in the middle of the lake.

I gave a technical presentation at the University of Manitoba and met some business and church people. Impressed by North America, I still did not have any clear idea about immigration at home. Meanwhile, the Cold War was heating up in Europe, and my sister felt that I would be vulnerable as a chemist in case of a Soviet intervention. Then a fateful event happened which actually made my decision: the communists built the Berlin Wall on August 13, 1961. On that Sunday, as we came from church and listened to the radio news at noon, I said to Magdalena: "That's it!" and I began to pursue systematically our family's immigration.

How do you start such an endeavor? There were three factors in my case: a sister in Canada, my employer already active in the USA, and my blind mother, who lived with us. So we corresponded with our Canadian relation, I talked to my employer, and we had family discussions with our mother. In addition, I corresponded with Canadian authorities in Ottawa, who sent me pertinent information on the country and employment. This established contacts but did not lead to a concrete job offer. One of the statistics from Ottawa showed that most immigrant scientists and engineers moved ultimately to the USA, and so I opted for the short cut.

My employer was initially receptive to my suggestion to work for them in the USA, but as 1963 came along they definitely dragged their feet and made no clear commitment. Meanwhile, our mother and the family council agreed that she would move to Winnipeg, and the Canadian Consulate in Cologne granted her an immigration visa. My sister picked her up, and they left by boat from Bremerhaven in May of 1963. On board ship I asked mother how she felt about moving to Canada. She replied that she was in God's hands wherever she lived and at peace with all. Then a brass band played a popular folksong about someone leaving his hometown while his girlfriend stayed behind. As the sentimental tune declined, the ocean liner gently steamed towards the North Sea and the Atlantic Ocean.

However, the Atlantic was everything else but gentle. It pounded the ship with house-high waves, so that it was in real danger. Even then, mother stayed calm while she prayed, and elemental fury was transformed into tranquility. My sister reported that an elderly lady kept looking at our blind and faithful mother, wondering how anyone could be at peace in danger and blindness. Mother and daughter knew why. They landed in Halifax, Nova Scotia, then took the train for days through several Canadian provinces to Manitoba.

Coming home from Bremerhaven, I felt anxious and frustrated. Mother's immigration was to precede my own, but there was no movement since the company continued to delay any decision. Our oldest daughter would start school next year, and we wanted to start her in America. I stayed my course but had no wind in my sails. There was a good position in Germany, but none known to me in either Canada or the USA. The old country had good employment offices including an international office, but it provided only professional positions in developing countries. Finally, in a telephone conversation, they brought to my attention some discrete information about American employment possibilities for scientifically trained people. I pursued and proceeded with the required paper work and received a total of eight potential job leads within a few months, including three concrete offers, of which I accepted the most attractive. Such was the professional employment climate in the 1960's.

My first visit to the U.S. Consulate in Frankfurt was on Labor Day 1961, when it was closed, the hard way to learn about an American holiday. My new employer would pay for our fare and even our modest household goods. Our savings could be used for starting a new life in America. Magdalena went along with all my decisions, but the burden of responsibility and potential risks was often heavy to bear. I wrote down my rationalizations, the pros and cons, and also read much on the USA and Canada. Ultimately, nothing else mattered but the decision itself. How can one decide without knowing, and how can one know without a glimpse into the future? Obviously, faith entered into this decision. In prayer I wondered about God's will. I remember one lonely winter hike in the hills above our hometown, when my mind was sore from stress by controversial thoughts and emotions. Finally, the decision was made by submitting my resignation on December 27, 1963, at the last moment, since my employment contract required a three month notice.

My prepared listing of reasons for our immigration included:

- The Soviet's political/military threat of Europe, which I took personally. War or communism were both possible and unwelcome.
- Europe's high population density.
- The desire to own a home soon and to escape city life.
- The desire for a professional change.
- To be close to mother and family in Canada.
- The children's future seemed more secure in America. In fact, I was convinced that our immigration would not just serve personal but family interests for a long time.

However, it is fair to add to these main ingredients a grain of adventure, a cup of longing for a spacious new world, and an ounce of independent spirit. One reason so typical for millions of American immigrants I did not have to list: we did not immigrate for want.

The three months before our immigration passed quickly, but they were stressful and I was glad when they were over. There were too many goodbye parties, visits, and journeys. After our furniture was picked up, we spent two weeks of family vacation in the Westerwald Hills, where the church had a wonderful home. Our children became quite friendly with the largely elderly guests, and we did a lot of hiking. At one point, though, a panicked thought struck me: What if this whole family would perish in a plane crash? But there was God-sent Mrs. Wolter who said: "Just step into that plane for America. Everything will be alright." God bless her in His eternal home after a life "which was only suffering."

When we finally left our apartment, I could not resist leaving the family's stuffed, black monkey on the attic railing in the old family residence. In due time, it would cheer up our good neighbors when they would hang up their wash. Ambulance sirens were in the air to pick up neighbor Armbrecht, when the taxi took us to the station, where father Winkel looked with pain at his departing children and grandchildren. We took the train along the beautiful Rhine valley, stayed one night in Frankfurt, then flew across the Atlantic via London and Newfoundland. Our official entry was in New York on April 8, 1964. After much delay, we reached our destination late after midnight. Our two cute daughters, with small canes and suitcases confidently stepped into the new world.

THE FIRST YEAR

"When times are good, be happy; but, when times are bad, consider: God has made the one as well as the other."

—**Ecclesiastes 7:14**

Immediately after our early morning arrival, I began my work in the USA at eight o'clock. How many doubts, how much perseverance and tension preceded this event! A certain hardness with self and others was associated with our immigration. People with whom contact had ceased long ago came and said goodbye. We will never forget the old house in Germany, the spot of family happiness for two generations, which we left, apparently unsentimental, since a well-rounded part of life had come to an end. Our immigration was not typical for the millions that sought the American shore. Even though it was well planned and executed, I was still surprised how smooth it turned out to be, easier than a move from one section of a German town to the next at that time, considering the housing shortage. Of course, adjustments had to be made and accepted.

The first days were stressful, when we had to calm down our tired children in the hotel, and then looked for housing, exposed to a hot and humid climate. Friends from work helped us in those early days. We went to (Emory Methodist) Church on Georgia Avenue since we could walk there. Of the extensive merchandise on that street we bought only necessities. We visited the city and countryside, were impressed, tired out, refreshed and happy again with our little family. President Kennedy was assassinated in November preceding our coming; he had been much loved and mourned in Germany. A respectful visit to his grave site in Arlington was one of our first goals, so the four of us stood in line at the grave overlooking the capital after walking with our two and five-year old children from the mall all the way across Memorial Bridge and back.

I liked my work, although I was not yet assimilated. Considering the easygoing American way, I felt tense amidst the newness around me. Strange surroundings did not surprise me. The country, its dynamics and people, the adventure of an unknown but predestined life kept me fascinated. We made many new acquaintances, met people of various races, origins, and occupations. We thought about observations not easy to understand, in particular America's social problems, which were more severe than those of Western Europe, but not nearly as harsh as they are now. Not affected by them, we bought a small house after three weeks in the USA, which for economic reasons was more attractive than renting. But for the next three months, we stayed in a furnished apartment. I closely watched the real estate lady as she sold us the house and was wondering whether or not I could trust her. We had no experience, had never before owned a house, and my English was too poor to even understand the sales process. Well, I trusted her, with no regrets later.

Uplifting, but also potentially hazardous, are success and progress. On May 19, 1964, I drove for the first time in America. We bought a rather new car. Coming from a VW Beetle in Germany, I was wondering whether I could drive "such a big vehicle," although it was only a compact car. Magdalena got a vacuum cleaner and a little transistor radio, which lasted more than a dozen years. We discovered a recreational park with its railroad and play area, highways, Washington, Maryland, Virginia, Timber Lake, and Great Falls. One of our daughters discovered that there are such things as teeth and saw a dentist. At her birthday she learned to ride a small bike. Later she also joined the kindergarten class at school.

Our Canadian nephew suddenly appeared at our doorstep. He came by motorcycle and he helped us move into our house in Maryland. On July 1 arrived our household goods, which we had not seen for months, everything boxed up on one truck. Exciting unpacking began, and our house became a home.

Soon thereafter, mother broke her hip, at her age of much concern. So we all drove up to Winnipeg via Chicago, Tomah and St. Paul, and reached our goal after 48 hours. The vastness of the USA and Canada almost overwhelmed us, as if we dared ocean crossing by canoe. We visited mother in the hospital. Her suffering was modified by confident joy, and she fully recovered in due time. We also found time to swim in Lake Winnipeg. Impressive was Manitoba's wheat covered space. Our return trip in two and one half days was via Kenora on Lake of the Woods, International Falls, Lake Superior, Mackinaw Bridge, and Pennsylvania. When Hurricane Hilda moved into Louisiana, we called Magdalena's Dutch relatives in the area, but they were not affected.

One incredible experience during the first year was meeting Paul [Paul and Harriet Klose; Jeff and Colet] and family at Thanksgiving, a relative in our small town. What a small world! Saint John's Church received us as members, and we met a lady from Germany in a sad family situation. Everything went smoothly with us until Christmas time, when our younger daughter [Monika] got sick with a rare blood allergy. Dealing with doctors made Magdalena use her limited English confidently and effectively. The Lord helped the doctors recognize the rare affliction, which later disappeared. I must mention that my English also improved, last but not least by reading the *Washington Post* despite my limited vocabulary, and by watching TV. We bought our first black and white TV set. 1964 was an election year, and we thought television would be helpful to learn something about the political process in America. Thus, our eventful first year provided countless opportunities for adjustment.

Happiness has many formulas. One may be America. But stronger is the comfort and covenant of a merciful God, joy in and evidence of His magnificent creation, and the loving understanding of a good wife.

FROM HOTEL MARYLAND TO MANITOBA

"Now about brotherly love, we do not need to write to you, for you yourself have been taught by God to love each other."

—1 Thessalonians 4:9

Our first Christmas day in America was unusually warm and sunny. So we spent time outside. On Sylvester day, we looked back on the first year in America, beautiful, sunny America with children's laughter, but unsolved social problems. Our garbage men were black Americans. We were immigrants from a former enemy country, yet enjoyed a house, yard, and comfort, which they might never experience. It perturbed me, and my heart went out to these hard working men.

On New Year's morning, we went to Great Falls Park. In the afternoon, the lonely lady from Germany visited us again. She was hurting so much, but all we could do was listen and be friends. In the evening, we saw Paul's family. His father had immigrated in the early twenties by jumping ship. Like my cousin Richard in Queens, he had roamed the oceans on a German merchantman, and then chose to stay in harbor. The authorities caught up with them during the war, when they were already loyal residents and provided legal papers. In March, I visited Richard and family on the way back from Boston, where some people collected cigarette butts from the floor of the railway station, as German smokers did immediately after the war.

The year 1965 turned out to be quite interesting. We painted two bedrooms and paneled the recreation room just in time, before our house became a hotel, as our friend Ilse and our parents Winkel from Germany, as well as our relatives and mother from Canada visited us. My sister, husband, and daughter brought her by car at Easter time, and she stayed with us until October. We knew Ilse from the church in Germany and a youth group trip to Scotland in 1952. Now she was helping Philadelphia area churches during Vacation Bible School. A very unique person, she was credited with teaching Spanish speaking kids from Puerto Rico English Sunday school songs with a German accent. The Winkels came by boat to New York, where we picked them up in June. They stayed until the end of January 1966. We enjoyed those good days in Maryland with both our parents. Father Winkel and I did also some extensive traveling to see his half-brother Sigfried.[24]

Sig had immigrated to the wilds of Manitoba right after World War I, when his father told him: "Son, there is nothing left in Germany. I'm going to buy you a one-way ticket either to Australia or Canada." Sig chose Canada and became a courageous trapper and hunter, later a fisherman with his own little trawler on Lake Winnipeg. I corresponded with him already from Germany. Now I wanted to arrange a reunion of the brothers after forty-five years.

We followed a carefully executed plan, since we had to drive 2,500 miles in order to catch a boat that departed only once a week. We left Maryland on August 19 at three a.m. for the Pennsylvania Turnpike and ultimately Seney in Upper Michigan, via Houghton Lake and Mackinaw City, a total of 884 miles. Our gas was depleted when we continued at five next morning and barely dragged the car into Marquette on Lake Superior to fill her up, as they just opened at seven. Then we drove through endless forests to Duluth, Minnesota, accompanied by an old hitchhiker. From there we followed Highway 2 via Grand Rapids to

---

24. Recall earlier story "The Servant of the Sick."

Highway 59 and Thief River Falls to Winnipeg, where we arrived at 7:30 p.m. on a most beautiful summer day and also Magdalena's birthday.

August 21 we spent on Falcon Lake, swimming and blueberry picking. Next day was Sunday, and after church we visited a German immigrant family from our hometown church. Then came the long-expected departure for Berens River. On August 23, our relatives drove us to Selkirk on the Red River of the North, from where the *Kenora* left with us around 6:30 p.m. Father Winkel and I sat on the upper deck as we slowly approached the lake. Millions of mosquitos danced in their own clouds on the banks of Red River. The serene river passage concluded with the setting of the sun, as a purple sky crowned Lake Winnipeg. Night's indifference to contours and colors swallowed lake, ship, and people into northern vastness. We slept well in bunk beds, then washed our sleepy eyes before the crew served an early, hearty breakfast.

In the morning of August 24, the weather was grey and stormy. Protected by my sleeping bag I watched the shoreline from deck through my large monocular. Our ship needed a pilot to steer it through rain and rocks, which blocked the entrance to the Berens River. After twenty hours, we tied up on the pier of the Hudson Bay Company and Indian Reservation. Father Winkel (74) did not recognize his brother immediately. He was smaller and older looking, although ten years younger. After forty-five years, two brothers sat united on the pier for our photo. We left by motorboat with Aunt Kay to have lunch at Sig's place. She served chicken and pork, and a farmer couple from southern Manitoba joined us. Kay herself was from a farm, before she learned the trade of hairstyling and met Sig while on vacation in Berens River. They married late in life and had no children. Their place consisted of a comfortable, green-painted residence, four other buildings, and an outhouse, all built by Sig, who even made the boards with his saw, then used saw dust for insulation. There was an icehouse. Others served storage, boat, and net repair needs. Kay had a large vegetable and flower garden by the river. At the pier, we saw the large "gas boat" used for fishing. On the property were also a freight sleigh, a covered snowmobile, a sawmill and other equipment. A sleigh-cabin with stove could be used for ice fishing. Kay served coffee and cake, and we listened to their life story of trapping, hunting, and fishing. She said: "I never liked the trapping."

There was the story about bear hunting, when Sig came to the banks of a river, spotted a huge black bear on his hind legs, concluded the bear was too tall, and wisely left the scene. At another time, he had left his rifle in his tent when bear pups came along. He put himself flat on top of a hut while a furious mother bear searched for him and destroyed the tent. Another person in the Yukon Territory was in his outhouse by the river when a powerful bear paw transferred both into the water below. But moose and bear were killed at other times. I slept on the porch, where a dead moose would be stored later as meat supply for winter.

August 25, 1965 was cold and windy. We went to the (Hudson) "Bay" for mail, saw a new Indian house (provided by the Canadian government for $25.00, visited "the Swede" who lived across the river with his Indian lady and was moving a house onto a new foundation, and "the East Prussian" who guarded supply buildings of the Icelander's fishing company on a large rock. Later we visited Mrs. Kamp (84) in her large log house. Well informed by radio, the only communication means up north, she recalled with distaste the Berlin Wall. Next day, we cast lead sinkers and degraded them to prevent damage to the nets. We visited a Catholic mission: French-Canadian sisters, brother, Indians, church, chapel, shrine, movie theater, hospital with X-ray equipment, a small power station, and covered snowmobile. Add friendship, cake, coffee, storytelling, a magnificent view over the bay with its rocky outcrops, wind and vastness, and put one sister with a white malamute into this landscape.

Later, we took the boat through coffee-colored water upstream twenty-five miles into the wilderness. A spare motor was on board, since damage by rocks was possible and nobody would pick us up in case of mishap. We came to waterfalls in forests with knee-deep moss. A fire served against the cold. By morning, rainwater was frozen on Sig's gasoline drums, but I dipped into the river as usual. We met the Indian agent and development officer and saw a portion of the empty beer bottles, which Kay picked up to pay for occasional boat trips to Winnipeg.

On sunny August 28, Father Winkel and I canoed to the edge of the lake, and I swam. Sigfried took me later to the East Prussian and to the Icelander Sigerdsen. Over whiskey the men discussed fishing licenses, nets, and credits. Since everything was bought on credit, all fishermen were dependent on the Icelanders, who had developed these northern parts.

On Sunday, August 29, our boat took us to the United Church, and Pastor Gordon Craig in his muddy shoes and clean, black robe. The translator needed many words in place of Gordon's concise English. A moving prayer was heard, as the Indians were reluctant to take communion. After the pastor said that Christ died not for "good" people, they slowly came forward, weeping over themselves and God's painful way of saving us, the unworthy. When the pastor's wife invited us and others for tea, we met a quiet half-Indian lady in her thirties, who only wished and waited for a white husband. No others may apply. In vain she waited for years. Oh simple, scenic world with not so simple solutions to problems of human purpose and identity.

SUPERIOR

"As the heavens are higher than the earth, so are my ways higher than your ways and my thoughts than your thoughts."

—*Isaiah 55:9*

We spent about two weeks in Berens River. Meanwhile September had arrived with early autumn storms. The *Kenora* was at Norway House up north and could not resume her trip south on Lake Winnipeg. A tempest in a large water bowl, and this shallow lake had become quite dangerous. In fact, a few weeks later, a similar boat was to sink near Hekla Island, with loss of life. Radio contact with the *Kenora* revealed uncertain late arrival in Berens River. For days I went to a river bend to scan the bay with my binoculars and felt like Robinson Crusoe. When she finally came in sight, I had to hurry to alert Sig, who would taxi us to the pier for a hasty goodbye, and for the brothers' final embrace. Sig would die in his beloved Berens River only four years later, in 1969, and father Winkel died in 1976. Our time is short and much more precious than we think.

Hardly were we on board when the *Kenora* left for Selkirk. It was a Friday shortly after noon, about the last chance to get going and back to work on Monday, 2,500 miles away. One more enjoyment of northern vastness from the top deck, one more night, on board, and one more hearty breakfast on the way to Selkirk, a twenty hour trip. But how would we get to Winnipeg from there? Nobody knew when we would arrive after the storm. Bless now the heart of Mrs. Margaret Green of Minneapolis, who had her car parked near Red River in Selkirk and drove us to our destination. We had to go shopping in downtown Winnipeg before we could take the Nova on its long trip to Maryland. That afternoon, we drove to Upsala, Ontario on the Trans-Canada Highway and spent the night, the next day along Lakes Superior, Huron, Ontario, and through the mountains of Pennsylvania to Maryland, one long day and night. On Monday morning, I was back to work on time.

Despite our hurried mode of travel, we were not insensitive to the scenery of the Great Lakes. Storm clouds moved over Lake Superior with its rocky islands, a majestic sight. The loneliness of Old Woman's Bay reflected open space and depth of time. Who are we, one-on-one with God's creation? Why not spend time in this oasis of solitude away from man's turmoil? I understood Sig's love of northern Canada. I understood his flight from city and commotion. But was he happy? Did he escape the troubles of life? Did he resolve his grudges with the past? He was still taking sides in insignificant personal quarrels that happened decades ago. Would I be different in solitude? Is isolated life possible at all? Are we not meant to be social beings, with interdependent life and support lines? Stern and powerful was the impact of Lake Superior's north shore on my mind. Each time I visited its shores, the mile-deep lake filled me with awe, even though, in perspective, it was only a puddle, with me like a grain of sand.

FELLOW WORKERS

"I went down to the potter's house, and I saw him working at the wheel. But the pot he was shaping from the clay was marred in his hands; so the potter formed it into another pot, shaping it as seemed best to him."

—Jeremiah 18: 3-4

All my life, I have enjoyed technology and laboratories. Technical details of such enjoyment and challenges are described elsewhere and omitted here, since they would interest only a few, and since they are solely rational, unlike our human lives. I came to the USA in the time of the Cold War, when other European professionals came over, too, with many of whom we socialized. Meanwhile, European living standards improved rapidly, and the one-directional flow across the Atlantic tapered out. On a positive note it provided to the country talent and to us opportunities and a convenient adjustment to America. Of course, most fellow employees were born in America including my boss, who was female. This was surprising news, and I really should not have wondered about it, because I was married already. In time we became friends, and being the heir to an old family estate with considerable farm land on the Eastern shore of Maryland, she invited us there. Her family had come around the time of Lord Baltimore, and now she entertained our children with pony and buggy. She also arranged the rental of a beach cottage for us in 1967.

Kind and honest, she always gave me good advice, while she kept smoking like a chimney. Sadly, this led to emphysema and early retirement in Florida, where she later died.

The kindest personality probably belonged to an older gentleman, who rode a BMW and co-owned a small BMW dealership. With my coworkers, a lady and a gentleman, I developed an excellent relationship. Both were black. The lady would have cleaned my test specimens, but since this kind of work would be demeaning, I was sensitive enough to do it myself. That way we remained very good friends. She was an excellent seamstress and took me shopping for a sewing machine and invited us to a fancy fashion show in the home of a well-to-do black couple in NW Washington. This was a distinct honor, since Magdalena and I were the only white folks there. Never before had I seen such a fine home and so many elegantly dressed people. Our friend is now retired; I hope for a long and happy time.

[I remained] connected with my friend Joe, a long friendship which lasted until his death in 1989. I visited him at home and met his wife. He took me and father Winkel on a tour of Washington and told us all about its black neighborhoods. "People always lived well together here. There, people never got along with each other. I don't understand why." Both neighborhoods looked alike, neat and middle-class. Joe loved to play baseball and laughed heartily. He went through hard times during the Depression, although things got finally better for him during the Roosevelt years. The government was then already far ahead in terms of remedying past problems, certainly farther ahead than American society as a whole. I think that race relations were generally better than portrayed by the press, although deep down some white prejudice simmered and sometimes seeped through the surface. Who would have believed in the troubled sixties that the white foreman of the shop, after a fishing trip, held his tanned forearm against Joe's to prove that he was darker, and both laughed heartily?

As the USA was sliding into the Vietnam War, some young ROTC officers were given employment, all smart young men, well versed in technology, and patriotic, up to a point. None of them opted to serve in Vietnam. One told me that he was too valuable with his technical training. No wonder that we lost that war. Not even the elite showed any commitment. But I admit that a patriotic atmosphere prevailed during the successful Apollo missile launches.

I presented a paper at the annual meeting of a professional society in San Francisco and flew out there in April 1968. At this occasion I had several interviews which led to two invitations by firms in the Midwest and to a solid job offer in Illinois. There I started to work in August 1968. In San Francisco the news of Dr. King's murder reached us. As I went back to the hotel, I noticed the frustrated look on the face of a young black passerby. The sad news in my adopted country affected me too. There was more frustration elsewhere, and fires flared up in America. I decided to take the bus across America in order to see much of the country. This took several days and nights: from San Francisco to Reno, Salt Lake City, Denver, Omaha, Chicago, Toledo, Pittsburgh, Baltimore. Over the weekend, I delayed my trip in Denver to spend time with friends from Washington. Chicago was tense, and Baltimore was dangerous, but the large, peaceful countryside between the Pacific and Atlantic Oceans belied the cities' social unrest and the newspaper headlines.

When the country was in turmoil, the actual country was in deep peace. Such is the advantage of continent-size space, compared to the tinderbox, crowded condition of the small, urbanized European states. In the summer of 1968, Magdalena took our two-year old son on his first trip to Germany, and I took the girls to Winnipeg. After my return from a 5,000 mile round trip, I got ready to drive to Illinois, where we had bought a house. The family flew in a few weeks later, when the furniture arrived. In the unfurnished house, resting in a sleeping bag on the carpet, my transistor radio informed me about the Soviet invasion of Czechoslovakia, a hateful repeat of the Berlin and Budapest oppressions in the

1950's. As it turned out, my industrial experience in Illinois had its pros and cons. On the positive side, I got into an interesting field that was to occupy me for decades, I volunteered and advanced in the Chicago Section of a professional society, and I found many professional friends. On the negative side, we experienced recession, reorganization and a difficult work environment. There was a lay-off in 1970, done in a rude way, and even though I was personally not affected, I had to address professional uncertainty for the first time.

In early April 1971, our Canadian niece Hanna married Bruce in Winnipeg, and we all went there by car. We drove through a quiet night, Magdalena and the girls in their sleeping bags resting in the back of the Nova station wagon and our son on a board above their feet at the rear window, a picnic container on the seat next to me, the driver. Such was our mode of travelling. My mind went into meditation, reflecting on uncertainty versus security, when I saw the vision of a peaceful, far extending path in the dark night. This gave me assurance that God would make our ways straight. I took a catnap on a field in Minnesota, and we all enjoyed a bright, sunny morning breakfast in outdoors North Dakota. In Winnipeg I found Norman Vincent Peale's book on "The Power of Positive Thinking." Never before had I thought about life and God with such encouragement. Now, I realize that some people don't like the "theology of positive thinking" and criticize it as manipulative. I could not detect that Peale was trying to manipulate the Almighty, but he helped me see in a practical way what faith can accomplish. Well, I came home to Illinois for professional advancement, and there I needed all the positive thinking I could muster. We were in a recession, and I had to interview people seeking employment. Thus, I found out how they were treated by their former employers. One of them lost his lab job in a well-known paint company after twenty years of service. Obviously, times were not only difficult for individuals, but also for companies. So, I held on to my job for the sake of my family and the loan on our house. But I also recalled my well-paying, secure situation in Germany and the treatment of professionals in that country, and I was wondering whether I should return. There are so many options in life. At a crucial time, good advice is precious. It was your mother, the most European member of the family, who said, 'You really love America and would not be happy in Germany.' I will never forget her unselfish position. Thus, in due time, I met other good fellow workers in America.

OF THE CAPTIVE VARIETY

"Trust in the Lord and do good; dwell in the land and enjoy safe pasture."

—*Psalm 37:3*

"Here we do not have an enduring city, but we are looking for the city that is to come."

—*Hebrews 13:14*

From the beginning, our immigration was designed like a one-way street. It would have been too disruptive and senseless any other way. Consequently, I pursued citizenship of my chosen country when I was six years in the USA. With two witnesses I went to the naturalization office in Chicago. I had attended classes on the Constitution and our government so I could answer pertinent questions. Without doubt, I felt like an American citizen, and I wanted to participate in our elections. Also, I felt strongly about the Western world versus communism. The citizenship council of Chicago invited me and others to submit essays about our experiences in the USA, and I wrote a persuasive article, which included my firm belief in freedom. This led to a special celebration with other new citizens, who were recognized a few days after the swearing-in ceremony. This ceremony was already special, as people of many different countries jointly pledged allegiance to the USA.

The elderly judge addressed the audience in the courtroom. "America is a demanding country," he said. "You must have experienced some bitterness in the past. Put this behind you for a new beginning." Thereafter, the city of Chicago gave a reception for the new citizens with coffee and other refreshments, and a choir from AT&T in blue and yellow uniforms sang several songs. Thus, I became an American of the captive variety.

It was a sunny, May day when Magdalena and I came home. From the house waved an American flag, and our neighbor Jack came over to greet me. "Say, Horst, what is really different since you are a U.S. citizen?" "Look at it this way," I replied. "Yesterday I was just plainly married. Today I'm married to German girl." At the time, Magdalena was not yet ready for citizenship, and I respected her decision.

Our daughters became citizens in Buffalo in 1976, the bicentennial year, ten years later than their brother, who was born a U.S. citizen in Washington, D.C. His mom joined him in solidarity after twenty years, when he served as a West Point cadet. Have I ever regretted my decision? No. Did I face difficulties or misunderstanding? Yes. Do I miss Germany? No, except for friends and relatives. Am I indifferent about Germany? No, I have only good wishes for the country that gave and took away so much. Germany's past has concerned me deeply, and so does America's socially chaotic present and her future. Here I am, an American citizen of German background. Someone in the world may meet me with skepticism. It doesn't matter, because I love this great country and the One who looks justly through all prejudice, even provides rain and sunshine for the just and unjust, so that they may change and learn to live with one another constructively in peace. Am I dreaming? This is the true meaning of citizenship.

IN THE NICK OF TIME

"Surely there is a future, and your hope will not be cut off."

—*Proverbs 23:18*

My work and residence were forty-five miles apart. Initially I drove to work, three to four hours each day, in part bumper-to-bumper, quite miserable in winter. Besides, the car would depreciate at the rate of 22,500 miles/year. So, I decided to take the train to the city, transfer to suburbia ["subway"], and walk from there 40 minutes to my employer. I got up before five in the morning. We drove to the small town's train station. At seven I arrived in the city, forty minutes later in suburbia, and ten after eight at work, which officially began at eight thirty and lasted until five. At night, it was the same in reverse. The workday added up to fifteen hours, except for the days when I missed the regular train. That was easy to do. The city's train system was built for left-side traffic by British engineers. The train came from the right, usually to the platform. The suburban station had suffered arson in the riots of 1968. Cold winds swept the platform in winter, when I scanned the bent of the tracks for the bright light of the locomotive. Lo and behold, on some days the train was not on the track to my platform, but to the next one, separated by a chain-link fence. So, I ran to the end of the fence and around it. Barely would I catch the end of the train or miss it.

When I came home, the children were already in bed, as they were in early morning; I did not see them until the weekend. My situation could only be justified by a good or pleasant job. Since it was neither one nor the other, the time to act drew near. But with the country again in recession, even a poor job was precious. Walking the final stretch in the morning, I crossed the bridge over an expressway, then turned right by the church which displayed a saint's sculpture up high. His hand was raised in blessed encouragement or patient caution, as if he would say: "Go ever slowly, but then with decisiveness." That's what he said to me for months every morning.

At the small town's station[25] I found a small Christian leaflet with a storm-tossed tall ship and the encouraging message that the Lord helps us in the nick of time. My inner being was storm-tossed, too. I was even contemplating to return to the old country. In fact, the consul reassured me that a return was a definite option. By correspondence, I discussed the matter with a good friend. I had also contacts with multinational firms. But my dear wife, even though European minded, said: "You really don' t want to live there again," and right she was. My personal and professional future was linked to America. I called the president of an Eastern firm, was invited to an interview, and accepted their job offer. Compared to the depressing atmosphere before, they seemed to roll out the red carpet. In the nick of time, the good Lord straightened our ways. Of three options (moving closer to the job, get a job closer to the house, or move elsewhere to new house and job), He chose for us the best option and guided us to a fulfilled life elsewhere.

---

25. We lived in Crystal Lake, Illinois at the time. I recall dropping my Dad off at the train station very early one morning in complete darkness except for some tall light poles that cascaded light on the double-decked, yellow and dark green-colored train cars.

CHURCH IN AMERICA

"You will know how people ought to conduct themselves in God's household, which is the church of the living God, the pillar and foundation of the truth."

— 1 Timothy 3:15

The gospel came to America via Europe and there via Asia. After the apostle Paul, in a vision, had followed the call of a man in Macedonia, the churches of Philippi, Thessalonica, Corinth, and Rome were founded, little house churches in the beginning. Not until the fourth century A.D. began a more formal church organization in Europe, particularly in Rome, the center of the empire. Augustine, in the fifth century A.D., contributed most after Paul for the spread of the good news. The empire and the church split later with centers in Rome and in Constantinople from where the Eastern Orthodox Church derived. Russia and the Ukraine received the gospel before America did, about a thousand years ago. After the reformation in the sixteenth century, two main theological orientations influenced the West. Each came over to America in due time, first with the Spaniards, then with the French, the Dutch, the British, and others. The Spaniards came to Florida and to the California coast, where their missions force-fed the Indians, and they ran away from the not so good deeds that accompanied the good news. The French experienced also a hard sell with their Indians, and even suffered martyrdom. One missionary, who stayed with the Indians in their smoke-filled long house, reported to his superiors in France that these poor wretches spend their life in smoke, and their eternity in fire.

A Protestant church of Anglican faith came first here in 1609. Immediately it was severely tested in the colony of Jamestown, Virginia. It is interesting to note that soon thereafter a variant of the traditional church entered America with the pilgrims in Plymouth, Massachusetts. Thus, from the very beginning, America experienced a proliferation of Protestant churches, which later mushroomed with the arrival of many nationalities from Europe and their various forms of establishment on the huge North American continent. Besides, for the Protestants the Reformation never ended. Up to our days they have kept splitting their churches. No wonder that the world is confused. It is also understandable that there must be a separation of churches and state in America. There is, of course, also another aspect of the multitude of Protestant churches. All churches are extended families, and each family is naturally different from the next one. One has to allow for individual expression. If only the overall unity would not get lost among the majority who agrees on 95-99% of faith and form issues, but may differ on 1-5% of other details. This common bond is frequently recognized and has led to common action and activities. Despite its fragmentation, there is much good to be said about the church at large.

So, when we came to America, it was not hard to find a church, or was it? For generations, this family went to church on Sundays and often also during the week. Such was family tradition in Germany and with Magdalena's Dutch family in Holland, and we wanted to continue it. Of course, it was more than a tradition. It was the realization that we need God while going through life. As mentioned before, in Washington we went with our little girls to a Methodist Church on Georgia Avenue, a white congregation in an all-black neighborhood. The members had moved to the suburbs but came back to the old church on Sundays. Our choice was not based on color or denomination. We simply chose a church we could walk to while we had no car. When we moved to Maryland, we were able to walk to church again. The services of this Lutheran Church were more familiar to us because of our background. Soon we became involved in activities; Sunday school, youth, choir, and church council. As a delegate of the Church, I attended the Maryland synod convention in Gettysburg, Pennsylvania. When Magdalena's parents came to visit us for half a year, father Winkel became quite active in our church, participated in the adult class, and even preached to the congregation. Our son was baptized in that church. A young minister on special assignment with the synod stood up and said there should be closer fellowship among the members of the congregation. So, he founded Koinonia groups. Initially, these were attended by many church members. There and then we began our friendship with the Poleys and Shillings, which has now lasted for thirty years. In a Lutheran church in Illinois we made friends again, including the Rogers, the Johnsons, and DuWayne Sheldon, who had lost his wife to cancer and was left with two young children. Our friendship began when we reached out and invited them. This church organized small groups, too. One focused on the subject of forgiveness. Once a month, a nice potluck dinner served the need for fellowship. At a fine camp on Lake Geneva in Wisconsin, available to our children and other youth, we spent a short family vacation.

After moving to New York State, our children were confirmed in a local Lutheran church. I received liturgical deacon's training, participated in communion, served on the church council for several years, was chairman for the bicentennial celebration (1976) and for the 75th church anniversary in 1978. This was somewhat ironic considering my background and the foundation of this church by Swedish immigrants in 1903. However, their descendants needed someone to organize such events and found in me an enthusiastic volunteer. One Sunday, I decided to hike in our beautiful hills before the service. Trouble was that I got disoriented and did not know for sure which way I should descend, while the church members waited for their anniversary assignments. Finally, I came home just in time to drive to church and meet the people as they emptied the church. I apologized to the pastor for missing the service, because I was lost in the woods. Laughingly he replied: "I never heard this excuse before."

The local Lutheran church with its fine congregation possibly still would have me as a member if several events and influences beyond my control had not interfered. Our daughters, through friends and college, found other church groups, and Magdalena started to attend services elsewhere. She, and later I, were impressed by one community church in particular. So, we went to this dynamic fundamentalist church as a family for the next five years. Magdalena was most happy there. She became Sunday school superintendent, and I taught the adult class, whom I jokingly complimented, since they never caused any disciplinary problems. We made many friends, gained much in Bible knowledge, and gave presentations to church groups. However, I really wanted to support our neighborhood church, where I served already as long-term treasurer, and where we could walk rather than drive sixteen miles one way. We belonged to this country community anyway, and I wished to support it fully. This was reasonable, but we had to make a concession regarding its form of worship.

I write down these details to show how complicated church life in America can be. This process provided an opportunity to become more informed and tolerant. It also became evident that form, rather than substance can be divisive among various churches and committed people. The insight we gained through this process allowed us to mature and learn to accept people the way they are. Of course, church people are not necessarily "easier" people. In fact, secular people at work or elsewhere may be more to our personal liking. But it's the church that does good in a cold world, and church we are committed to. There are, of course, many direct benefits. First, our faith is not so much a theology as a way of life; a most positive, constructive, realistic way. It helps us to become less selfish, more generous and willing to reach out to others, who, in turn, may reach out to us. We are guided into better choices through faith and rearrange our priorities, which leads to my next story, portraying the man of Nuts, Incorporated.

THE MAN OF NUTS INCORPORATED

"Seek first His kingdom and His righteousness, and all these things will He give to you as well."

—Matthew 6:33

A nice-looking man, successful businessman,
Cracked nuts, sealed and sold them in cans.
Fantastic business; Grew in leaps and bounds.
So he said: "I'll build bigger warehouses,
Store nuts for years to come, and live happily
Ever after."

But the Lord said: "You fool, tonight you'll die
Of a heart attack. Who will then own these nuts
And the whole business?"
A hard verdict, when he had the chance
To enjoy life?
Is anything wrong with working hard for a living,
With establishing successful business,
With retiring, enjoying life?
Three times NO.

So why is he called a fool?
First, he was quite selfish
And wanted all nuts for himself.
Look at his jaws to believe it.
Second, he had no place for others.
"Let them work as hard as I did
To get what I have.
I'm not in the sharing business.
I'm in the nut business,"
And he became a nut himself.
Third and mainly, no place for God.
"God is unpractical
In the competitive nut business."

Ironically, he went to church.
The songs they sang were very soothing.
He did not seek first
The kingdom of God,
His righteousness.
All those nuts, the whole business
Could have been added unto him.
He built the business for himself,
And lost it all that night.
A nice-looking man, successful man,
Ignored God,
And missed the purpose of his life.

"OLSON, HERE IS TOLSON"

"God is our refuge and strength, an ever-present help in trouble."

— Psalm 46:1

What did Vietnam, winter weather, and a car have in common? The answer was "trouble." In the afternoon before Thanksgiving Day, I left Chicago-land for Canada. Since road ice potential and low temperatures were predicted, I prepared myself with chains, two sleeping bags, a foam mattress, and a well-stocked picnic container. It turned out that I would need all of these items. Around Madison, light-freezing rain began to fall. So, I admitted a young hitchhiker for additional weight. He was immediately helpful in putting the chains on the wheels. We had good conversations, although from diametrically opposed positions. He was an antiwar radical and draft dodger, while I considered the Vietnam War as necessary Western defense. At that time, other people's sons were serving the country in the military and the University of Wisconsin had its share of radicals, and even experienced a bombing that killed one person in the math department. The man's ride with me ended in St. Paul, from where I drove into the night. Wet snow made driving miserable, until I came to Sauk Centre, where Sinclair Lewis of "Main Street" fame was born in 1885. The northern country was just cold. Snow covered only the fields, not the roads. A good catnap refreshed me under the clearest star-lit sky I ever saw. There was our galaxy, the Milky Way, and there the

North Star. It became my guide on the lonely journey through isolated, quiet villages. In Alexandria I stopped after midnight and arrived at my sister's home in Winnipeg in time for breakfast.

One afternoon, while my mother, family, and I shared coffee and cake, severe weather for Manitoba was predicted. So, I decided to leave immediately for home, located 814 miles to the south. Travelling on dry and lonely Highway 59 just before dusk, I noticed that my car ran steadily slower. More gas made no difference; the vehicle rolled until it stopped. Hardly any cars shared the road with me during the last hundred miles, but at that moment a pickup truck with three young men pulled in front and soon towed me into the next place of habitation with the nylon rope I carried along. Here, on a Saturday night, I was left in the dark at an unattended Mobile gas station. I had been through Ogema before, one of those places where you are in and out by the time you read the sign, and it reminded me always of alpha and omega. Since I belonged to the American Automobile Association and the service station was AAA affiliated, with a small residence behind the pumps, I expected help. But everything remained dark and indifferent. It appeared that Ogema just consisted of the highway, the gas station, and a few dark houses on a side street across the road. Occasionally a drunk and loud music emerged from a tavern at the corner, until the very cold air quickly drove both inside again.

As I pondered upon my slim options, walking up and down, I finally crossed over into the side street. Perhaps one of the houses would show light, and someone could help. A few cars were parked below the deep sidewalk. In the dark I noticed a man behind his steering wheel. There I explained the situation. "Come with me," he said, "we'll call the service station." Down the road we entered a sober-looking building with a telephone inside. "Olson, here is Tolson, we are here in jail. Could you help this man?" I was already wondering about the unpainted plywood interior with several padlocks. "Just go over there again. He will be with you in a moment." Thus the town cop Tolson got Mr. Olson out of bed around eleven. Olson was not too kindly inclined, but looked under the hood. "It's probably the coil," he decided and found one that might fit. "You have to wait for the mechanic, but tomorrow is Sunday. It's up to him whether he wants to come in." Then Mr. Olson went back to bed. So did I, in sub-zero weather, in the station wagon with the mattress and two sleeping bags. It was quite comfortable in there, although not like the Hilton, at least better than the public housing Mr. Tolson could have offered. Next morning, a friendly mechanic from Detroit Lakes came twenty-five miles north to help me. It was a worn mechanical distributor with metal filings inside. A replacement was not available. So, the capable man blew it out with air, lubricated it, and advised me to go not faster than sixty-five. I gave him a good tip and made it safely home. Thus the good Lord was my ever-present help in car trouble, by mobilizing a total of six people on my behalf. Mr. Olson was not quite right when he said, "If you travel in these parts during a winter night, you are on your own."

There is an epilogue to this short story, since Ogema was much more interesting than I had imagined. When the gas station was opened at six in the morning by Mr. Olson's brother from Moorhead, some customers stopped, and there was this orderly lady, who waited for her father. Around seven, loud and disconcerting arguments in the residence could be heard. Finally, the Olsons stormed out and dragged their daughter with them to the Catholic church, where she did not want to go, before they drove her back to college. Then arrived the nice lady's father, who had spent the night in Mr. Tolson's care after drinking, gambling, and losing money among the Sioux Indians, and she gave him a stern look. Lack of discipline is an American shortcoming with long roots. Actually, they reach back, in military terms, to the Continental Army and Valley Forge, where General von Steuben helped correct the situation. Greed is another one, as my late black friend Joe so vividly stated one morning while we drove to work in Washington: "This country is money-crazy." Now he would also say, "this country is gun-crazy." But that is a separate story.

THE PEACE GARDEN PISTOL

"The Lord will keep you from all harm; He will watch over your life."

—Psalm 121:7

The many wonders of this world may be as diverse as the North American continent and the institution of family. There is room to roam, and it may open your heart wide, especially if you come from a small or crowded European country. There is also room to maintain a close, caring family relationship. These were the two reasons for my most memorable automobile trip in the early seventies. My youngest daughter [Monika], then ten and a half years old, accompanied me. She had not seen grandma for a long time. We did not know that we would see my mother, then eighty-five, for the last time.

Since my car had grown old too, I leased a spacious vehicle in the Chicago suburb where I worked. It was practically new, with only 3,000 miles on the odometer. We left around noontime of a Friday preceding the Independence Day weekend. In the bright afternoon we passed Freeport in the hilly countryside of northwestern Illinois, on our way to the Mississippi. At Dubuque we crossed the river and followed it north on the Iowa side, Guttenberg with its large Mississippi island glowing peacefully in the evening sun. As we continued our journey into the night, we drove into Minnesota, crossed the Mississippi at Winona to Wisconsin and our camping site on Lake Pepin, the Mississippi's large extension, where water skiing was invented. Our comfortable car served us well with its two sleeping compartments, front seats and back seats, during a restful night toward a joyful morning. No river panorama is more scenic than that of the Mississippi at Lake Pepin on a sunny summer day. We then travelled through the Twin Cities into northern Minnesota, picked up Highway 59 at Detroit Lakes for border crossing into Canada, and promptly arrived at the family residence in Manitoba's capital, Winnipeg.

It was obvious that mother had longed for us, although she could not communicate well. When I read her favorite passages, Psalms and Romans chapter 8, her heart was warmed, her nervousness calmed down. What can really separate us from the love of God? Indeed, the Lord was and remained her shepherd. After several days with her and family, we began our extensive return trip. For hours we travelled southwest through sunny Manitoba with its golden waves of wheat, our thoughts and prayers left behind.

The International Peace Garden straddles the U.S./Canadian border and includes over two thousand acres in the Province of Manitoba and the state of North Dakota. It commemorates peace between the two friendly nations, friendly also to our own families, at the longest undefended border of the world. North American peace greatly appeals to me, since I had been at the receiving end of war elsewhere at an early, tender age. It has also saved me many thousands of tax dollars.

Many ideas on peace are expressed in the Peace Garden's chapel. If implemented, let's say in the Middle East or in the former Yugoslavia, all these poor people could become independently wealthy fast. Alas, money is not everything, and peace is elusive. There is no peace without justice, no justice without order. Neither one exists in our selfish and chaotic world. Around that time, we came to the end of the Vietnam era, and peaceniks abounded in the world. With my anticommunist conviction, I was not one of them. Later, when I went with my Japanese friend Yosuki to the Atomic Bomb Museum in Hiroshima (one of the most methodically arranged places of sobering education), I was reluctant to write my name into the visitor's book, lest someone would mistake me for a peacenik, with his monopoly claim on love for peace. But in the museum I had seen the shadow of a person on the reddish stone facade of Hiroshima's Sumitomo Bank, all that was left. "What is your life? You are a mist that appears for a little while and then vanishes," says James 4:14. So I wrote, while recognizing how inadequate the expression is, "A necessary documentation," and signed my name. Gentle reader, you too have lived with the bomb since its, or your, existence.

Because it was my custom to buy picture postcards at interesting or scenic places, I drove to the Peace Garden's concession building with its small and crowded parking lot. I always locked my car doors, but not this time. After all, it was just meant to be a quick stop. As soon as I had entered the building, I felt uncomfortable with those open doors, and immediately returned to correct my omission. Looking ahead I noticed a man in his late twenties making hasty arm and body movements away from my leased car. He was still standing there when I arrived. I gave him a dim view, opened and locked both car doors, went back to get the postcards, and drove on.

My young daughter enjoyed the spacious park in the Turtle Mountains with lakes and playground by surrounding birch trees, a lovely sight. We descended from the hills into the flat lands of North Dakota. An Indian pow-wow was held just outside the Peace Garden. Then wide, open, largely uninhabited space engulfed us for several hours. We did not notice that the state steadily and significantly sloped upward from northeast to southwest. At Rugby east of Minot we passed the geographical center of the North American Continent. As a rest stop we selected the sunny, lonely banks of the Missouri River's Lake Sakakawea, named in honor of the Indian lady guide during the Lewis and Clark Expedition in 1805. It was the middle of summer, when one may expect other tourists. Yet the world seemed to belong to us alone. North Dakota then became particularly scenic and mountainous as we approached

Theodore Roosevelt National Park. A group of horses and riders filed slowly across the road by the Little Missouri River in the late afternoon sun. The Park's North Unit provided our camping site. A friendly ranger told us about the local flora and fauna, while a single buffalo peacefully grazed nearby like some neighbor's cow.

In the morning we followed Highway 85 toward the South Unit of Theodore Roosevelt National Park and the western town of Medora, made famous by the Marquis de Mores, speculator, cattleman, and nobleman. Before the Park's entrance was an overlook above the North Dakota badlands, a very colorful sight. The colors stem from eons of erosion and the baking action of sub-surface coal veins, slowly burning there for centuries. This was a worthy object of photography. So I reached for the camera. It bothered me that the protective cover for the wide—angle lens was missing. It might have fallen down below the driver's seat. When I reached down, lo and behold, there was a pistol. While we toured the Park and enjoyed its stern, scenic beauty, I was pondering what to do with the unwanted weapon and where it came from. I could have thrown it out of the window. At one point, when I looked from some bluffs deep down to the Little Missouri River and its lonely northern course, I considered throwing it there, where it might not be found or harm anyone for a century. But better judgment prevailed. I went to the rangers and told them that I found a pistol in my leased car. At once a ranger came out with paper tissues and got the gun. He looked for fingerprints, took six bullets out of the drum and went on radio communication. His scrutiny soon found that the pistol, a so-called Saturday night special, was never used. "You can have it," he said, "and you did the right thing by bringing it here." Finders, keepers, but I declined, since I never wanted to own a weapon, with its potential to quickly inflict irreversible harm. My attitude did not hinder my son from becoming an expert on infantry weapons, and I'm quite comfortable with leaving pistols and guns in the hands of our military, police, and responsible hunters. Yes, it was risky to do the right thing. I noticed a smirk on the head ranger's face, as he apparently imagined foul play, which undoubtedly he had seen before in his profession.

Where did the pistol come from? I ruled out family and all circumstances on this trip, except for the suspicious encounter in the Peace Garden. Could I unknowingly have leased the pistol with the car? This is unlikely, too, considering prior service of the leasing garage. Whoever put a loaded pistol under the driver's seat had the sinister intention of sitting there to use the weapon quickly at will, not likely a case of losers, weepers. But with us it was a case of finders, winners, who had avoided harm and were able to move on into the greatest landscapes I was ever privileged to see. Never will I forget the incredible scenery of and around Highway 85 through South Dakota: a straight, black asphalt strip, flanked by yellow sweep clover on both sides, for hundred miles, pastel colors left and right, lonely rocks and distant mountains, blue sky, bright sun, nobody there but us, and somewhere an unattended flock of sheep. Then came the Devil's Tower of Wyoming into sight, Black Hills, Mount Rushmore, Bad Lands of South Dakota, Pipestone National Monument, Prairie du Chien and the Mississippi, wonders of this world.

EXCELSIOR

"You will not fear the terror of night."

—Psalm 91:5

"There is where you will stay overnight, conveniently close to the air-port," my friendly associate advised. We could clearly see the Hotel Ex-celsior as we landed, stretched out, modern, grey, without visible lights, and vaguely gloomy. After a pleasant, long, hot, and humid day, it was meant to be my resting place where sound sleep would recharge my bio-batteries for an early morning departure to the continent. Fire en-gines had converged in front of the lobby, but soon drove off when we arrived. "Let me handle this alone. You must be tired," I offered, but my friend insisted on helping while I was checking in. At the desk, a tall lady could not find my reservation, looked up briefly, then assigned a room to me anyway, Room 1322. What gave me the idea that something sin-ister was in gestation? Suddenly a heavy lady excitedly requested some information from the check-in person. A distraction? I walked across the crowded lobby and took the elevator to the third floor. Part of the floor was only dimly lit. Despite the late hour, a maid stood there and asked whether I would need any help to find my room. I found it myself after walking along a lonely floor. There I applied the safety key to the electronic lock and, once inside the room, bolted the door. Why did I have such an eerie feeling? The door chain consisted of a series of rings.

The largest at the end was to hold on to a small, split ring at the door, but was difficult to insert. A little plate within the chain rings finally allowed to conclude this procedure. Hardly had I settled down around midnight, when the telephone rang and a female voice asked whether room services were needed. They were not. Television programs were as unimaginative as elsewhere, except for vile and violence. It was really time to tune off and turn off television and lights, my mind still wandering while winding down.

"Hello, hello, helloo?" A soft, male voice at the door repeated itself, "hello, hello, helloo?" The time was one A.M. "Hello, hello, helloo?" the voice persisted. This was going on for ten to twenty minutes. Although wide-awake, I did not get up. "Hello, hello, helloo, I am a C.P.," the voice concluded with a strange claim of assumed authority, followed by the sound of safety key sliding into the door lock. As the electronics responded, the door handle was pushed down. However, the entrance to the room was blocked by the door bolt. What is a C.P.? Before I could speculate, my telephone rang with determination, remaining unanswered with counter-determination. This case looked like an orchestrated effort by a duo or trio, with headquarters right in the hotel. Thereafter, the frustrated criminals seemed to retire from targeting me for robbery, and I fell soundly asleep. I could have called the police, but their investigation would have robbed the rest of my short night. Next morning, when I advised the manager that her hotel was crime infested, she seemed to be more concerned about the unsecured lock of Room 1322 than about its recent occupant. Excelsior is the comparative of excelsus, Latin for high. A Higher one, in fact the Highest one, had looked after me that night.

THE TENT IN THE MOUNTAINS

"In the heavens He has pitched a tent for the sun, which is like a bridegroom touring forth from his pavilion, like a champion rejoicing to run his course."

—Psalm 19: 4b-5

Comfort and convenience never persuaded me to like hotel or motel rooms, except that they kept me off the street, albeit not necessarily safe, as shown above in the Excelsior. Some hotels provided a lot of comfort or luxury like the Hotel Qkura in Tokyo or various great hotels in California. Yet there is only a subtle transition from hotel guest to prisoner in a golden cage. Nowhere was this more evident than in Nagoya near Kyoto, where the choices or location were limited to a crowded street scene or a narrow room, with a slither of visible sky to make the confinement more unbearable. I would rather stay in a simple North American camping area, where you enter into a realm of freedom and the manager could ask you, "how do you like your coffee?" before he assigns a slot on the grounds under tall southern trees. Perhaps such attitude goes with immigrating from urbanized Europe into the boonies, because it offers room to roam. As elaborated in a Western song, "Don't fence me in."

Wave after wave of wooded mountain chains and green luster surrounded the yellowish colored tent with our small group of family campers. This was not even a developed camping area, but a spot of secluded immersion into nature at high elevation. As the sun was setting, the cooking fire became a warm campfire while my harmonica entertained our ears and added to our hearts' contentment. Admittedly only mildly musical, the player's missed tune enhanced our feeling of belonging and provided an atmosphere of soul before soft moonlight descended on the tent. Nothing exceeds sound sleep in fresh air, so close to mother nature. A whippoorwill woke us up in the morning to a day of active leisure. With no escape or regret possible, why doesn't anybody perfect the alarm clock by using the energetic bird's voice?

Activity is not in contradiction to leisure, idleness is. Francis Parkman filled my leisure time with meaningful and easy reading. France and Britain competed for supremacy on the North American continent. The Bostonian wrote the extensive history like a fascinating newspaper account of yesterday's drama. Add peace, quietness, extended views and sunshine, and you have a perfect recipe for relaxation. It lasted a whole week, a sweet taste of true freedom. Why can it not last forever? Both free and dependent, we long and we work. We should convert work into leisure, keep our spirits at ease, dependent on God. There was time for reflections. After difficult months of professional pressure, I felt how my penned-up stress gradually left body and mind.

Occasionally we all need the seclusion of a tent in the mountains. Our physical world "rests" at equilibrium, with all forces in dynamic balance. Regarding international affairs, Thomas Paine said, "The balance of power is the scale of peace." Excessive heat and humidity got us out of our comfort zone, "unbalanced" us in order to stimulate our lives. Such external factors let us search within the realm of remedies. Our family swim in the valley's stream was the right answer. A good book, a campfire and harmonica, scenic views and singing birds help put life into perspective. Now even memories of the tent in the mountains put a soft touch on the soul.

THE VANTAGE VIEW[26]

A steep incline
In bright sunshine:
Step by step,
I walked the length
Of my path
With added strength
In quietness
And confidence.

A wide vista
Opened in solitude,
With fields and
Forests to show.
A clear creek below
Reflected gratitude,
Flooding my heart
And mind.

Way high, a blue sky
With cirrus clouds:
Fair weather doubts.
Your ways are high,
Higher than ground
I ever found.
Superior thoughts
I never knew.
Oh, grant me, Lord,
Your vantage view.

---

26. Dad shared in a letter, with love, "HWR, 9-19-95".

ANCIENT MOUNDS

"Yes, and from ancient times I am He. No one can deliver out of my hand. When I act, who can reverse it?"

—Isaiah 43:13

A river was the separating line between the city of the dead and the city of the living, the latter long gone, the former in front of us, as if death was the ultimate constant. Pre-historic Hopewell Indians and the earlier Adena people were preoccupied with death and afterlife. On the banks of the Scioto River in Ohio, they built the mounds of Chillicothe, burial mounds with tale-telling gifts: a mica-hand, where mica is not available; a copper helmet, actually a skull cap of the metal found on the distant Keweenaw Peninsula, which points like a finger into Lake Superior. Obviously, there was far-reaching trade in America, also superstition, and a vague longing for eternal life.

Thousands of mounds dotted the eastern half of America, all the way west to Oklahoma and the upper Missouri, always close to waterways, like villages along a road. Many were leveled by subsequent farming. Thomas Jefferson in his younger years described finding a mound on family land, where he did a systematic archaeological cross-sectional study. Not all mounds were used for burials, but all had religious or sociological significance. Some belong to the interesting group of effigy mounds, some formed like birds or bears. The famous serpent mound near Hillsboro in southern Ohio is a quarter of a mile long, shaped like a local snake, with a mysterious oval shape or egg by its mouth. Bluffs along the Mississippi carry many animal symbols, seen, for instance, in Effigy Mounds National Monument near Marquette Iowa, across the river from Prairie du Chien, Wisconsin. Half way between Madison and Milwaukee, near Lake Mills on the Crawfish River in Aztalan, a Wisconsin State Park, are stockaded mounds created by intruding cannibalistic folks, who were understandably very unpopular with their neighbors. Were they possibly distant cousins of the Aztecs, spreading north on the Mississippi, Wisconsin, and Crawfish Rivers? Or were they just spiritual relatives? Near Cairo, Illinois, at the confluence of the Ohio into the Mississippi is the huge Mound City, and in Moundsville, West Virginia, a tall cone-shaped mound. We have seen all these sights, except for Mound City, and reflected about the past, the peoples' lives, their meaning. With few answers on abundant questions, many mysteries remain.

Our favorite mounds are near Cartersville in northwestern Georgia, on the Etowah River. Chieftain's houses and huts once occupied the top of some Etowah mounds, while happy village life played itself out along the scenic river's bank. Somehow we imagined children's laughter there and contentment, like so many irreversible scenes on the stage of fleeting human life. One can sense the grand design of it, and the proprietary claim of each group of people, the various mound builders in America, whose special memorials we inherited.

THE ISLAND

"He will not falter or be discouraged till He establishes justice on earth. In His law the islands will put their hope."

—*Isaiah 42:4*

Before holiday breaks, our German second grade teacher let students read exciting stories to the class, among them Robinson Crusoe and his island adventures. Although fascinated, I could not imagine that I would ever spend time on an island myself, certainly not in faraway Canada, or without the feeling of being deserted. Robinson's island was just a small speck of land in the sea. That a huge island would exist within a lake was beyond my comprehension. But such island is real, with a thousand miles of shoreline and large lakes within. Needless to say, surrounding this island must be a Great Lake. Its name is Lake Huron. Besides Manitoulin and other islands, it also has room for more than 30,000 rocky islets.

Manitoulin Island can be entered by bridge or by boat. The northern access is off the Trans-Canada Highway near Sudbury and leads to the North Channel, which separates the island from the mainland. Here one of the rarely seen bridges, which turns on a pivot, alternatively allows car traffic across the bridge or the passage of sailboats with high masts through the channel. The southern access is by ferry from the rocky tip of Bruce Peninsula at Tobermory to South Baymouth and Manitoulin's gently rolling hills. There is still a respectable Indian population that reaches back into prehistoric times. Archaeological evidence indicates that Manitoulin Island was already a favorite hunting and fishing spot 20,000 years ago. Both geography and history make Manitoulin interesting, but its recreational features have the greatest visitor appeal.

Providence provided our precious experience with Providence Bay. Formed like a large horseshoe facing south, its sandy beaches were flanked by low layers of rock. Gentle waves rolled in and over frolicking children while a light breeze moderated the sun's steady touch. Combine this with a spacious and well-landscaped campground, and you are not really surprised to encounter only happy faces. Relaxed strangers may talk to each other at the beach, alternating sun bathing and swimming. The area is also a fisherman's paradise. Personally, I am on the side of the fish, in particular when served with French fried chips.

At the island's far western end is Meldrum Bay. The old light house keepers used to spend here most lonely days and nights. They also encountered dangerous situations when they tried to resupply themselves over the ice with their oxcarts. A vacationer came out of a secluded house to get his mail, amazed to see our eastern state's license plate, there "at the end of the world." This area featured extended smooth rocks, like a natural highway, honed by glaciers' ice ages ago. From the black sheets of lava further west, one can see Cockburn Island, only a short distance away. On these sharp lava rocks, La Salle's *Griffin* perished in the fall of 1679, as some people claim, based on certain shipwreck findings.

Rene Robert Cavelier of Rouen made four memorable voyages to North America. During the first one (1666-1674) he went from Canada to discover the Ohio and Illinois Rivers in 1669. The French king, Louis XIV, then elevated him to the ranks of nobility as Sieur de la Salle. During the next two voyages (1675-1677 and 1678-1682), he became an even greater explorer, but also a master negotiator and trader. He was then governor of Fort Frontenac, which was built in 1673 at Kingston on Lake Ontario. During the winter of 1678/79, he built Fort Niagara at the mouth of the same river, and a little later Fort Conti near the Niagara River on Lake Erie. There his master craftsman, Hillaret, built the *Griffin*, the first sail ship on the Great Lakes.

In August of 1679, La Salle and company sailed through Lake Erie toward the current site of Detroit. Arriving there on the name's day of a saintly lady, La Salle named the local body of water Lake Saint Clair. They sailed then into Lake Huron, discovered Saginaw Bay, and landed on Mackinaw Island with its already established Indian trade. After paying a visit to the Jesuits at Saint Ignace, La Salle explored the Green Bay of Lake Michigan and traded again for furs with the Indians. The *Griffin* was now heavily loaded. La Salle had planned to continue toward the Illinois River and could have used the ship for transportation to southern Michigan, but he was also hounded for his debt by merchants in France. So, he decided to send the *Griffin* back to Fort Conti, with the intent to unload and get the merchandise transferred to Forts Niagara and Frontenac. The ship was then to return immediately, and to go to the St. Joseph River in southwestern Michigan. Meanwhile La Salle and subordinates would canoe along the unknown western shore of Lake Michigan, while his trusted army captain Tonty would do the same along that lake's eastern shore. Eventually, everybody including the *Griffin* would rendezvous at the St. Joseph. The *Griffin* left on September 19 from Mackinaw Island and was expected to be in southern Michigan within three to four weeks. La Salle expected to make his canoe trip in about 14 days, but actually needed 40 days because of fierce storms on the bad-tempered lake. Tonty was expected to arrive first at St. Joseph, but came in second, since he encountered even worse weather plus starvation, whereas nobody ever saw the *Griffin* again. It was fall time. Yet within the three groups of travelers, no one knew the awesome side of the Great Lakes. A mariner once told me that he considered them potentially more dangerous than the ocean, because of their waves' bathtub reflections.

As La Salle proved to us on Manitoulin Island, there can be much more to camping than meets the eye. He went to the Illinois via the St. Joseph and Kankakee Rivers, then made the trip to and from Canada two more times, before he canoed down (and later up) the Mississippi to its delta to "found" Louisiana in 1682. After his return to Canada and France, he organized his final trip to North America (1684-1687). It showed La Salle's boldest vision and would have been the capstone on his decisive claim of the American heartland. With four ships, future settlers, women, and children he sailed via Haiti and Cuba to the Mississippi Delta but overshot the target toward Texas at the Matagorda Bay. There they were stranded and endured terrible hardship. One ship did not even make it to Haiti, one deserted, two others perished at different times, but ultimately a small group found the delta and travelled north, sick and deeply divided, until La Salle was murdered, only 44 years old, one of the great founders of America, who predestined the Louisiana Purchase.

Is the mysterious disappearance of the *Griffin* really linked to Manitoulin Island? Why would the ship have taken a northeasterly course on Lake Huron? Did stormy weather blow it toward Manitoulin? Was dishonesty involved regarding the valuable cargo? Did the crew plan to divide it among themselves at the French River junction east of the large island, where traders converged? We had time to ask such questions. In unexpected ways, an island visit can sharpen one's focus. Events and people before us have a greater impact on our lives than we may think.

HIGH DUNES

"How precious to me are your thoughts, O God! How vast is the sum of them! Were I to count them, they would outnumber the grains of sand".

—*Psalm 139:17-18*

Wind, water, sun, sand, the shrill cry of gulls, hard walking, and protection are for me the mental connection with dunes. Think of the North Sea, the oceans, Atlantic and Pacific, the latter everything else but pacific on our West Coast, but also consider the great North American Lakes, associated with names like Lake of the Woods, Winnipeg, Superior, Michigan, Huron, Erie, Ontario, and many others. Sheltering dunes protected us from wind at Lake Winnipeg's Grand Beach and at the world's longest fresh-water beach, Wasaga Beach on Lake Huron's Georgian Bay.

Dunes obstructed our anxious views of large bodies of water but provided excellent vantage points once we climbed to the top on Virginia's Chincoteague Island or at South Carolina's Huntington Beach. Usually just one continuous wave of sand, and not too high, dunes are certainly no mountains, except for the Sleeping Bear Dunes, among the biggest sand piles of the world. Interestingly, this pile of sand is not located at the sea, but on one of the Great Lakes in the northwestern part of Michigan's lower peninsula. What a mass of silica particles to be counted!

Crystalline silica, alpha-quartz, four-hundred and eighty feet above the green waters of Lake Michigan. Chippewa Indians named these dunes after their legend of a bear and her two cubs who swam across Lake Michigan. There is South Manitou Island with its lighthouse, forest, and flowers, a good swim away from the coast. Ship traffic used to go through the narrow strait. Not every ship made it through safely, so a lifeguard station was placed nearby. High dunes with real long views, these ones are in a class by themselves, formed during ice ages, and still being formed by shifting sand. Ghost forests were once covered by the advancing dunes, then bleached and later uncovered again. Yes, there are wandering dunes, but the Sleeping Bear Dunes are too big to move out of the state of Michigan.

A walk to the top of a dune through shifting sand may be hard, in particular on a steep incline, reminding us of a hard walk through life. Rocky outcrops may give firm assistance, just as the good Lord puts our feet on a firm foundation. Sometimes we encounter manmade steps up and across a dune, provided by people that do not only look out for themselves. We are to be such people. Solid steps through shifting sand are taken in countless situations. Often we wonder how we ever got across some of the hurdles in life. It took just one confident step at a time, one day at a time, one after another into the future. Hope is ultimately realized. A grand view is gained.

SEASCAPES

"There is the sea vast and spacious, teeming with creatures beyond number."

—Psalm 104:25

"He stilled the storm to a whisper; the waves of the sea were hushed."

—Psalm 107:29

For years I longed to see two extreme geographic features, alpine mountains and the sea. I had to wait until my early twenties before I would get to the Austrian Alps, and one year longer to see the North Sea. Near the city of Groningen in Friesland, Dutch engineers had gained land from the mighty sea. It was late fall and quite windy. Fellow students and I were standing on and behind a massive concrete dyke, about five feet below sea level. Depending for dear life on a man-made structure is a unique experience. During a vacation at a later time, we crossed the 30 km long Barrier Dam between Friesland and North Holland, viewing the Waddenzee on one side and the Ijsselmeer on the other.

There were trips with a youth group across the English Channel between Ostende and Dover one August. Because of a still wind, the water got choppy, and many people were seasick. They had eaten pea soup for lunch. So peas were flying across the upper deck like bullets, and I had to duck and find cover, then worked myself toward the bow of the ship where the wind provided a perfect shield against flying vegetables. Plowing toward the white chalk rocks at Dover in sunshine, I enjoyed the wild and windy beauty of the waves, while my stomach never objected to the unsteady planks below it. We then travelled by train to Edinburgh and the Firth of Forth with its majestic bridge. At a later time and flight from Glasgow to London, I saw parts of the Irish Sea.

Other trips around the North Sea led to the harbors of Rotterdam and Hamburg with the upper Elbe river, also to Bremerhaven, from where my mother emigrated to Canada, while a brass band played a sentimental melody about leaving town and loved ones. A particularly good time in the North Sea region was spent with my sister in Zeeland at Kortgene and surrounding quaint cities like Goes and others. After the devastating storm flood of 1953, this area of large islands is now protected by a system of concrete dams, which connected the islands and created large lakes close to the sea.

I don't know how many trans-Atlantic flights I took over the years. West-east flights from North America to Europe seem to occur during nighttime, in the opposite direction during day time, often with clear views on a course through northern regions. Southern Greenland with its high mountains and glaciers became visible. Dependent on the time of year, a large flotilla of icebergs would sail down the Davis Strait into and beyond the Labrador Sea. Ninety percent submerged, only the tip of an iceberg was visible. One of them hit the new "unsinkable" Titanic in the fateful year of 1912. "Your sister Clara was born then," my mother used to say, "when the Titanic hit an iceberg in the night and sank with great loss of life."

On the day of our immigration, we saw Greenland, too. The weather over the East Coast was terrible then. We were diverted to Newfoundland and stayed at Gander for a few hours. On our way to New York and Washington, we flew over the Bay of Fundy. Years later we would camp on that Bay with its tides of up to 59 feet and the Moncton River reversing itself during high tide. We also camped and travelled along the Gulf of St. Lawrence, the Cumberland Strait, around Chaleur Bay and Cape Gaspe. The Gaspe Peninsula left a lasting impression. There, as it enters the Gulf, the St. Lawrence is ninety miles wide. For fifty miles, a lonely road without railing hugged the river on one side, steep rocks on the other, its potential danger only surpassed by incredible scenery. The coastlines of New Brunswick and Maine, Boston Harbor and New York, Maryland and Virginia all added to our Atlantic exposure. Swimming at a cove of Maine's Arcadia Park in August was like a thermal shock experiment for integrated circuits in the laboratory. The view from Cadillac Mountain over the sea was superb. But Champlain was not impressed in the sixteen hundreds. "Look at these barren rocks," he said on board his ship, then turned around at the inhospitable coast and sailed to his beloved Quebec.

The Chesapeake Bay is a very unique Atlantic extension, creating a peninsula attached by only some twenty miles to the North American continent. Cambridge is recommended for oysters. The states of Delaware, Maryland, and Virginia share the eastern shore. Assateague and Chincoteague Islands provide excellent swimming opportunities, sometimes among wild ponies. At a hot summer noon time, one smart pony of Assateague Island remained up to its neck in the Atlantic for two hours, with people swimming all around it, occasionally lifting its head to avoid salt water getting into the nostrils, at other times just floating with a swell. A long bridge-tunnel connecting the Norfolk and Cape Charles areas of Virginia granted long views of the Atlantic Ocean on one side and the Chesapeake Bay on the other.

Further south are the Outer Banks of North Carolina with Cape Hatteras and its black and white candy cane lighthouse. This "Atlantic graveyard" appears to be "way out toward Africa." After a hurricane, the manager of our campground said, "wind is not our problem, water is." Indeed, we saw washed-out roads south of Cape Hatteras. One of my favorite places on the Atlantic is Huntington Beach State Park in South Carolina. Early in the morning a large red sun was rising above the waters straight east, which appeared at an angle "of one o'clock" rather than "three o clock" relative to the coastline, because it ran from northwest to southeast.

The Gulf of Mexico provided superb beaches, and near Freeport in Texas also superb chemical facilities. Of course, a normal tourist would prefer only the former. Among the world's most scenic shore lines is North America's Pacific coast. The Big Sur and Monterey areas, Santa Cruz, Half Moon Bay, and northern California delighted the eye from an occasionally daring coastal road. An aerial view of Washington State's Seattle area showed many islands around Puget Sound, Olympic National-al Park, and the Strait of Juan de Fuca. After seeing America's mightiest rock, Mount McKinley in Alaska, there was a stop in Anchorage on Cook Inlet of the Gulf of Alaska, before our flight to Japan continued over the North Pacific Ocean near the Bering Strait. We visited also the Sea of Japan, cold and scenic. From Kagoshima on the southern island of Kyushu, we saw Mount Sakurajima smoking like one thousand chimneys. Ashes covered our heads when we toured the area, which became a peninsula in 1914 after a massive volcanic eruption. A ferry over the ancient and deep caldera connected us with the big city, whose residents begged that the wind would blow the ashes toward other communities. But everybody got his share.

So we all, friends and family, have received a temporary and partial share of the world's majestic seascapes to enjoy and to respect. When the *Arcadia* crossed the Atlantic from Bremerhaven to Halifax, Nova Scotia in the spring of 1963 with my sister and blind mother on board, they encountered a vicious storm in the North Atlantic. House-high waves pounded and endangered the mighty ship. At the table, which they shared with the captain, he conceded that he was not in control. During the fury of the storm, mother [Grandma Rauhut] stood on board unmoved. A fearful lady watched her in amazement. How could anyone, old, blind and helpless, be so contented and steadfast in the eye of a deadly storm? The faithful can, since they confidently trust in their higher power.

MOONSCAPES

"The heavens are yours, and yours also the earth; you founded the world and all that is in it. In the council of the holy ones God is greatly feared; He is more awesome than all who surround him."

—*Psalm 89: 7, 11*

Where astronauts treaded the black moonscape for training prior to their moon voyage in 1969, where lava rivers flooded the countryside as early as about 15,000 years ago, where mile-thick layers of lava were accumulated over eons, where ancient volcanoes had formed tubes, barriers, and other surface texture, there I would like to be again, not on the moon, but in the State of Idaho. A portion of the Oregon Trail led through the area in the eighteen hundreds, causing grief to travelers. When I drove through the area one hundred years later, I was surrounded by strange scenery and loneliness, not a soul in sight. What if this car would break down?

Standing on a cone-shaped hill of black cinder, my white shirt provided a strange contrast, while I was dwarfed by the expanses of Craters of the Moon National Monument. Cones of frothy lava were formed by molten rock, shot into the air by gas discharges. Some lava tubes are hundreds of feet long, and as wide as a railroad tunnel. Scant vegetation, such as a lonely tree between that cone and an extinct volcano at the horizon, came along only after volcanic activity had ceased for two thousand years. In some spots, which appeared uniformly black and lifeless, volcanism seemingly occurred somewhat more recently. Yellow flowers formed a decorative border around black, old, basaltic lave beds. Hikers are warned of razor-sharp lava and volcanic glasses. Certain trails are prepared for visitors, while cross-country, or better cross-lava exploration is discouraged.

Native people in America and elsewhere have claimed a spiritual relationship to the land of their ancestors, land that sustained, sheltered and surrounded them as long as they remembered. What a contrast to the refugees and rootless societies of our days, so often on the move, so often stopped in urban areas. Can roots be established through asphalt or concrete? I don't know whether ancient people claimed Idaho's volcanic land before or after lava beds covered it. A traveler feels a less emotional sensation than a native but cannot escape the aura of the land either. The moonscape is at the same time strangely repulsive and attractive, the closest experience to space exploration. Incredible space without people. Cosmic and earthly violence ultimately became the basis for fertile land and life. Everything in this universe mysteriously belongs together.

THE BOONIES

"Trust in the Lord and do good; dwell in the land and enjoy safe pasture".

Psalm 37:3

Nestled in our wide valley, the small community became home for many years. Warm light was shining through the stained glass windows of the old church when we first visited the valley. By now, our family has lived in its vicinity longer than in any other place. Country experience, scenery, neighbors, and church are dear to us. The male members of our family adjusted quickly to the spacious, scenic outdoor setting. It took a little longer for our ladies. Our girls missed old friends, suburban style and order. Even the trees on our road looked neglected. The church was built in 1892, but its history goes back to the early 1830's. Its flavor has changed over the years, but the message remains on target. Unique is the fact that this country church has stayed open, unlike so many others in America that became empty shells or disappeared. Our relationship with the [Haskell] Community Church has been immediate and supportive, and we appreciate the fact that we can walk to church. People are relatively poor, very helpful, and generally mind their own business.

Boonies are a kindly form of boondocks, rural backcountry, mountainous, sometimes wild in ways and weather. While now somewhat developed, we can imagine how wild these parts of the country must have been in the past. Sedimentary fossils indicate that a sea covered this area in the very far past. Since the higher elevations show the same fossils, we have to conclude that our mountains folded upward at a geologically more recent time. A river flows now six miles away from here, well-travelled by the Indians. The Algonquians used the river highway for thousands of years, and later the Iroquois. We know that the Indians hunted within a few miles of the river, since numerous arrowheads were found on certain hilltops. Also, a field not far from our house showed charred discolorations, indicating recurring campfires, perhaps a summer camp. All this came to an end in the early 1800's, when white men moved into Indian lands. They first settled in our vicinity around 1830. The valley was then covered with a fine growth of pine trees. So they literally cut their farms out of dense woods, built saw mills, made shingles, and rafted lumber. One settler got a break from nature when a tornado felled the trees standing in the way of conversion into farmland. He bought the land, went back east to get his bride, and was pleased to find his back-breaking pioneering work reduced when he returned.

Some settlers farmed on our hilltops, where hikers may still find old foundations or stone piles, up to 700 meters above sea level. Then they developed the area around their small farms. A blacksmith shop, two stores, a post office, even a hotel came into being, where the weary traveler could listen to the peepers during spring time. The first schoolhouse was built of logs, with cracks chinked by pieces of wood and plastered with mud on the outside. Students sat on slabs while warmed by a fireplace. Few of these old features are left in our community. But even with electricity, automobiles, and airwaves, the boonies are still with us, and with them a special way of life. Much space and quietness, exposure to both vigorous weather and sunshine, your own well water, independence from city services, a closer look at creation and the animal kingdom. We befriended some dogs in the valley and obtained our own four-legged friends. Our feeder attracted numerous species of birds unknown to us before. On fields and hills we met deer, woodchucks, porcupines, raccoons, grouse, and wild turkeys. These intrigued us in winter with their long arrow foot prints in the snow (which point into the opposite direction of their movement). Unforgettable moments, when we encountered two-dozen turkeys with their young ones on a sunny summer morning, when they flew up into the trees, or scared us by suddenly flying off.

Not everything is harmonious in nature, for instance the majestic hawk's way to survive and catch his prey. But mostly, every creature enjoys its presence without worry, the very moment of life. There fly wild ducks and geese, and high up in cruising speed two herons. The boonies are a hiker's paradise, rewarding him with far views and perspective, dreams of a better world, with wildlife observations, with peace, healthy exercise, and fatigue. No wonder that the dog went wild when he sensed my hiking boots. One hillside blends us in with hushes and high grass, humble souls in overwhelming scenery and creation. We find wild strawberries, raspberries, blackberries in abundance, and apples in unlikely places. Was Johnny Appleseed at work, who had walked these parts? Or are we on an old, abandoned farm site, before settlers decided to consolidate farms in the valley? It's a time of meditation, spiritual and physical recharging. The boonies are balanced, good-tempered, relaxed, not hectic. Like life, they are fragile. Could they survive a reckless march of mankind?

SILENT NIGHT
CHRISTMAS REFLECTIONS

"Fear not, for behold, I bring you good news of great joy that will be for all the people."

—Luke 2:10

Christmas was always a cherished celebration in our home. Some of my fondest childhood memories are of Christmas. My friends thought it a bit odd that we celebrated on Christmas Eve rather than Christmas morning, and we never quite reconciled how Santa pulled it off. The Super-8 movies are another glimpse, although partial and imperfect, into our Christmas. Most disturbingly, the movies remind us that the "good old days" weren't always that good. In particular, the clothes of the 1970s—in my case the large-collared, orange V-neck with plaid pants Mom thought were suitable—remind us that too much visual stimuli is distracting. But the movies reveal another side too; a real side that I now appreciate more fully as an adult and parent. One of my favorite moments is timeless footage of Mom holding a "deer spotter"-strength lamp that went with our Montgomery Ward movie camera. As Dad captures the highly illuminated Christmas Tree, he scans too far. He catches Mom by surprise; clearly pleased with neither the duty, nor Dad's obsession with his new toy, Mom's facial expression says all that Dad, and posterity, need to know. These moments speak silent volumes and remind us to live and enjoy the life we have been gifted.

Our custom was to go to church for a candlelight service at which *Silent Night* was featured, followed by a light dinner at home with German treats. We kids would go upstairs while my parents prepared the family room with candles and presents. The catalyst that set our home celebration in motion was when we heard our parents singing, "*Ihr Kinderlein kommet*" [Oh Come, Little Children]. We would spend some time at the living room piano singing Christmas hymns then move into the radiant family room in which the Christmas Tree, Christmas Pyramid (tiered, rotating Nativity display powered by candle heat), and other family heirlooms set the most reverent atmosphere. My Dad would read us the Christmas story from Luke 2, sometimes combined with elements of Matthew 1 and 2, then express how we had been blessed that year and how thankful he was. Each person, in turn, would do likewise until our excitement could contain us no longer. Like many, I have my own personal memories and can recall gifts given or received. By far, my two most cherished Christmas memories are of my parents. The first is of my parents singing *Silent Night* together, in German, both at home and at Church, occasionally with the addition of a recorder. The other reflection is of just watching my parents. I still see a tear or two welling up in their eyes as Dad read and as they shared their gratitude. As a young child, I just took it all in, not sure why Mom or Dad would be so introspective or even sad on a night like Christmas. Now I know. We continue these customs, the same tears welling up in my own eyes, especially after their departure and when thinking of how richly blessed we remain.

Through the years, Mom shared her immigrant stories with local schools, organizations, and church groups. Mom's childhood Christmas memories and traditions were often featured in her story telling. What follows are speaking notes which she used to tell this part of her story to a church group in 1979:

"Let me take you back with me so you can participate in my memories of past Christmases. Before we get into those though, let me remind you of another very unusual occasion. Let us envision the shepherds keeping watch over their flocks and suddenly they saw a great light and heard a message loud and clear so that they were afraid and the angel said to them:

> *"Fear not: for behold, I bring you good tidings of great joy, which shall be to all people. For unto you is born this day in the city of David a Savior which is Christ the Lord."*

May we hear this message anew again today. We, who are hurrying to and fro, who are involved in our homes, schools, places of work, college, in our community and church. We who are surrounded by people in grief, sickness, loneliness, despair, and disasters. May we be touched and awakened to celebrate in joyful remembrance the birth of our Savior Jesus Christ and go as "missionaries" to bring the good news because: "For unto you is (also) born a Savior which is Christ the (your) Lord!" And may we not stop at just this first good news; may we go and tell of the life and death of this Savior also and proclaim victory through his resurrection! Let us all be missionaries to those around us in our homes, towns, the street we live on, the churches we go to. Let us not only be hearers of the good news but doers also, let Jesus become your reason to live, your Lord.

The only reason I have the courage to stand in front of you here and talk is to thank Jesus that he was willing to come to this earth to bring us into a right relationship with his father and himself through his love and to acknowledge his guidance and protection in many different circumstances, so that the message became reality: "Fear not!" So let us just say I am sharing with you, I am not a "trained" speaker, may you see Jesus through me.

CHRISTMAS MEMORIES:

1931-1933: Didn't remember. Was in Indonesia. No snow so mother (Maria Blok) made snowballs from tin paper.

1934: Background…Holland: Nicolaus day December 5th; gifts exchanged on the 5th in the Netherlands rather than Christmas day on the 24th which serves as a spiritual holiday. Church services and festive dinners.

1935: Do not recall.

1936: Celebrated in Glauchau, Germany. Was 5 years old. Advent season (show calendar house and hung calendars)… huge house, spacious family room. First Christmas tree from floor to ceiling, real candles on the tree (show candle holders). Lots of music, learned to play the recorder (show with case). Gifts: Farmhouses, recorder with book, 30 pfennig doll from my mother dressed in a ski outfit, all hand made. Cookie plate with 1 orange, apple, and nuts.

1937: Forgot

1938: Recalled 3pm Sunday School Program. Celebrated at Aunt's house in Duesseldorf; great gifts; baby stroller; movie camera for cartoons. At home, small gifts. Father Winkel working on a pig farm because he refused to join the Nazi party. [Grandmother (Metzger) lived with us. Cannot remember Christmas Tree but we probably had one. Father's mom (widow India) remarried Metzger. 2nd Husband died. 1st Baby also died (to be named Magdalena)].

1939: First Christmas during war time. Dad home for a few days. Christmas tree started on fire, no problem. [pail of water @ Grandma's

house]. Always read the Christmas Story, said some poems or Bible verses, sang songs and then were allowed to look at our gifts which were on
a table covered by a blanket. Lots to eat and joy because of a promise of
no alarms [air raids].

1940: Second Christmas during WW2. All at home! Special treat: or-
anges, nuts, coffee for mother! Again: no alarm.

1941: Christmas in Glauchau again: Still lots of music, more depressed.
Son [of Aunt Gretta Meyner] in Russia [likely Gefreiter Christoph
Meyner, message driver in an air intelligence or signal unit, later killed
in action on 22 June 1942]; husband on the Western front [Dr. Ernst
Meyner, Sr.]. I without my parents and brothers knowing about the terror of bomb raids. Enough gifts, doll houses up again [typically the children were allowed to play with toys for a period, then packed up to be
re-gifted later]. Church services of course. Churches were always filled
at Christmas. Vacation from school of course.

1942: Camp [Bad Salzungen], Orders from government to celebrate
their way [had to sing Nazi songs, march]. Good leadership [...camp
leader liked me (11 years old by now). Let me sing some Christian songs
because I asked.]– Schmeigemarsch ("silent march") singing of Christmas songs—opening presents from home: Baby doll Bed and doll. Was
allowed to take to my room. Santa came also. [See letters Mom wrote to
Glauchau in Appendix!]

1943: Another camp [Freudenstadt vic Leipzig. Kinderlandverschickung (KLV). -Lager (Wh/30), Hotel Württenberger Hof, Freudenstadt,
Germany]. Hard work, not much joy; very homesick. Went to church
but felt very lonely.

1944: Glauchau again with her mother and brother [Gerhard]. Had small apartment, little Christmas Tree, a special ration of 2 buckets of coal for which my mother had to stay in line for hours and almost fainted when she came home with them frostbitten. My mother had knitted a pullover for my brother and sewn a dress for me. We also were able to save enough ingredients to bake some cookies. Father in Duesseldorf, Brother [Ernst] in the Army [Air Defense Artillery we think]. [Gerhard fled Glauchau at some point...he had fallen in with the Hitler Youth and came home one day completely disillusioned, calling them liars/deceivers. He threw his uniform in a corner, and his mom (Grandma Winkel) told him he had to flee, and he did so by bike in late '44 or early '45].

1945: War was over, alone with my mother in Glauchau not knowing anything about the rest of our family. [Left in the spring of '46 after Russians gave 24 hours to leave with no more than 30lbs of stuff].

1946: First Christmas after the war. All 5 of us back together again. Deep depression for many people who had lost their loved ones. Had even a Christmas Tree which fell and all the ornaments broke. Had made cookies; saved ingredients for weeks. Some flour, sugar, etc. Had 1 goose egg which counted for 3 eggs; pretty helpful for baking. No oven, so a Baker said he'd bake and burnt their cookies! He felt so bad that for weeks he gave them extra bread. Remembered just 1 gift—a thimble Gerhard [Mom's brother] found and wrapped for her (Magdalena).

1947: Still hungry and sometimes cold. No coal; father searched for wood in ruined buildings, etc. Brothers brought pails of coal; parents found out later they stole them from trains. Bible verse "Give me not riches, nor let me be poor, that I might not be tempted." Sunday school—handmade roller-scooters. 5-6 kids & scooters in train car which were usually filled with people. Hardly anybody had a car.

Christmas eve we went to sing in bunkers [former bunkers were used for the poor/homeless as housing], filled with homeless people. Some of us took people home. My parents always invited somebody lonely and usually it was somebody despised by most people.

1948: Christmas with my grandmother present [Grandma Metzger formerly Winkel]. Had to give up her apartment and move in with us.

1949: Grandmother had died; Aunt & Uncle [Tante Mimi & Uncle Martin Metzger the painter who was the first child of the second marriage] moved in with us. Desperate need of housing. Food was easier to get, still rationing cards; but enough at least compared to years before.

1950-1956: Each year got better. The trees became larger, the decorations more, the gifts fancier and wrapped in pretty paper. But did the real joy deepen? In our family, which by then enlarged because of engaged young adults, we always kept it simple and never left the songs or Christmas story out, but the thankfulness for just able to be alive, being together and at peace; [the joy] dwindled down and was taken for granted.

1957: First Christmas as husband and wife. Rented one room from my parents, had our very own Christmas Tree in a flowerpot. Husband came home for Christmas vacation; was still studying in Munich [PhD work].

1958: Own apartment, mother-in-law lived with us-blind but a joyful Christian in spite of losing her husband, 2 sons and a daughter during WW2! Parents came; brought again 2 lonely people. Food in abundance.

1959: First Child—a daughter a delight [Birgit]! Most impressed by the candles on the tree and the Pyramid (show Pyramid).

1960-1963: Second daughter almost 1 year old [Monika]. My parents with their guest. Singing and, of course, the Christmas Story. 1st Christmas Day all children & grandchildren at Grandparents house.

1964: First Christmas in the USA. Very lonely. Amazed about outside Christmas decorations. Disappointed about electric lights [on trees]. Monika was very sick, maybe leukemia? Invited for Christmas eve [by well-intended neighbors] did not want to go, thought you <u>had</u> to be at home with your own family. Went—surprise candle, etc. Stollen from Germany.

1965: Parents came from Germany, just like the good old times.

1966: 8 day "old" son; the joy was so real; a live Christmas Baby Boy [Mike]!

1967-1979: Much the same, like you probably. I baked Christmas-Stollen (German fruit bread), and tried to put 2 traditions in one great celebration.
Two Christmases were struck by losing a loved one:

1972: December 22nd my mother-in-law went to be with the Lord. So my husband flew to Winnipeg, Canada to be with his sister, and on Christmas Eve morning laid her body in the ground. We know, however, that her soul was rejoicing with her Savior and those loved ones she lost before. I was alone with the children but kept up our way of celebrating.

1979: I took my son home to Germany for what was supposed to be the Golden Anniversary of my parents, but the Lord took my father home through a stroke and Christmas was celebrated in grief for the man who was for so many years just past and leader of our Christmas celebrations. Because of his testimony for his Savior who he also accepted as Lord, we could sing with joy, *"O Holy Night."*
I shared quite a few Christmas celebrations with you and probably left a lot of details out, but what is most important to me is that you may see how God, or let us say the Lord, always keeps his promises…There

is hope for those who not only hear the Christmas story as we call it, but also believe the message of it. There is joy in the midst of strife, confusion, grief, sickness, loneliness, and even despair for Jesus came to find you! So listen one more time: "Fear not, for behold..." Luke 2:10-11."

JANUARY THAW

Snowflakes drift
Slowly, undecided
Through January sky,
Left and lost.
Clouded sky breaks
To flood us with light.
Great numbers of crows
Descent and cry,
Shrewd and shrill.

Blue sky, green Firs,
Harmonized colors.
Chirping birds
Fly swiftly
Over fresh grass.
Time is granted
To rest and talk.
Hillside peace frees
Our restless hearts.

Precious friendship
Will last forever,
While our tracks
Are embedded
In soft soil.
We aim high
And remember in
Laughter and joy
The Master's mind.

MARCH MEDITATION

This March again
Is stormy and sunny.
Colorful birds
Sail through blue sky.
Robins return
In great numbers.

But where are the grackles?
Way up on our pines
They screamed for nine years.
Why not during the tenth?
Canadian geese
Honk and fly North.

Bittersweet March
With its light
Reminds us,
As branches cast
Soft shadows
On untouched snow.

She came and went in March,
Through peace to freedom.

MAY FLOWERS

Light concealing,
Space revealing
Clouds grant us
Warm rain.

Colors forming,
Flowers blooming:
Joyful song's
Refrain.

Mutual caring,
Friendship, sharing
Lives and faith
Maintain.

Leaves emerging,
Hearts resurging:
Future, hope
And gain.

H.W. Rauhut
5-28-95

BEST FRIENDS

"A righteous man cares for the needs of his animal".

—Proverbs 12:10

Their ancestry goes back thousands of years, to China, ancient Egypt and the rest of the world. They hunted with or accompanied their masters, protected, saved or entertained them, proliferated into a great variety over the centuries, and are still with us as some of our best friends. Whatever their appearance, their eyes reveal character and loyalty, often humor, seldom anger. Their forgiving nature is without equal. Are they "only" dogs, or creatures on a friendship level that few of us can reach? They know how to live each moment of their short lives, not in the past or in the future, quite contended even under adverse circumstances. Each one displays special personality traits, but they also share behavior patterns developed over a long period of time.

Not until we moved into the boonies did we associate ourselves with our four-legged friend. He was still a puppy and lived with his shepherd mother and siblings at a campsite. When we arrived there, they all had spread out on an elevated platform, a sight of dignity and contentment. Then he arrived at our place, a happy, fluffy fellow who immediately took a doll away from the girls and led a lengthy chase around the yard. He was Fluffy, our good friend for eight years, never-fatiguing hiking companion, swimmer, snow-dog, with a chuckle in his heart. No one loved snow more than he. No one else could get enough of this white, cold, Fluffy stuff. No one else would jump higher to catch powdery snow or snow balls. No one but he and we would play the game of Toro in summer time, when he charged our waving sack cloth like a bull in a bull fight, resourceful and lightning fast. On a hot, humid day, the whole family took a swim in our creek across the road. Guess who was trying the backstroke? Fluffy. One time, during a bicycle hike, someone tried to grab my bike from behind. Guess who discouraged him quickly? Fluffy, of course, was dependable. I did not even look back. He also pulled the bike on level roads. There was only one major fault with him: he liked to chase cars, which could lead to complications when he tried to combine the former with the latter. Chasing cars finally led to a crippling injury and his death. When the hour came, he put his head on my hand in ab-solute trust. We cried like little children when he was no longer with us. Many memories he had left behind. A few years earlier we experienced an April snowstorm that blanketed our hills and invited a most mem-orable hike. There he stood portrait under snow-covered trees, his fine coat caked with his beloved white powder, his brown and black fur con-trasted by all the white around him. That's the way we remember him, our playful, beautiful, fun-loving friend of great strength and courage. His funeral under our tall spruce trees rendered us all empty and quiet.

Fluffy's successor was Samson, named for his strength and selected from a litter of Siberian Husky puppies for the vigor he displayed. His potential power did not hinder him from always showing us and visiting children his most gentle nature. Often, I took one of his fang teeth and moved his head with it, asking him about his dentist. All this and more one could do, without Samson ever losing his balanced composure. It is said that his Husky family members had stayed with Siberian tribesmen for centuries, who loved, cherished and closely befriended their dogs, outdoors and in their tents. Evidently such love rubs off. In due time, we became the beneficiaries of the long-gone Asian masters' healthy dog appreciation. They must have loved their friend's unique facial features, too. Few creatures look equally good.

Like Fluffy, Samson became a great hiker, always walking without a knapsack. Unlike him, he didn't like to swim, although he was quite capable of this sport, too. He liked cold weather. After a snow storm in late spring, he looked quite contented in his dog house, the tip of his black nose exposed to the wind, while he told himself that such weather is much preferred to summer's "monkey" heat. Rain did not discourage him either. Philosophically he observed from his doghouse's vantage point everything that moved on our lawn or was able to lay eggs elsewhere in our lilac bushes. Without further talk, one can learn from a dog, whose happiness was not dependent on the weather.

Strangely funny was Samson's vain attempt to catch rabbits. Fascinated with them, he slowly approached them like a tiger and came as close as possible without alerting their long ears. Then all of a sudden he ran and jumped. But these rabbits countered his straight move by a quick zigzag retreat in to tall grass. There he sniffed and pondered upon his unsuccessful chase, yet never learned from his experience. Not everyone will gain from experience in vain. Such limitation he made up with great musical ability, certainly more developed than mine, who is only mildly musical. Every so often during a cool day or at night, in particular when a full moon evoked certain strings in his soul, he bent his neck backward and sang the age-old song of his clan, a most melodic howl. Not only solo, but, also duo or trio performances were granted. Hilarious were our impromptu trio concerts at the stairs to the house. There we stood and sang, our voices raised toward heaven, three hearts with one soul in four tunes. This was concluded by sneezing, which he imitated quickly.

Samson left us too early, and we buried him next to Fluffy, eulogized by the obituary below.[27]

SAMSON, TEN YEARS OLD

Blue, sunny sky.
He jumped high
When we hiked.
He just liked
To be
With me.

As a pup still,
Climbing a steep hill,
He was after my heel.
We shared our meal.
Last month,
Last hike,
Same hill
A full cycle.

Warm, morning sun,
Another day of fun.
Joy and peace,
His soul's keys,
Eyes reflecting
Gentleness.
I'll miss
His look,
His voice.

---

27. Samson liked to sit on our front steps with his hindquarters resting on the top step, front paws locked on the step below. Tail wagging; he would wait in this position until approached. The singing commenced, all members of the choir standing or sitting on the steps. We concluded our chorus with sneezing; I would fake a sneeze and watch as Samson repeated with his own.

He sang with soul,
Out of his whole
Heart.
Whistled melody,
Strong bond
Between him and me.

Our wonderful
Friend
went.
Although
No longer Mine,
He's fine.

Two months later came Maggy, full-grown Labrador lady with a clean family tree, muscular and freedom loving, the greatest hunter of them all. We did not have much time to build a relationship, but she accepted us well and loved our boony environment with the creek across the road. There she would swim and cool her Labrador blood. On the morning before her accidental death, she seemed to look sadly at me. She deserved a better ending despite her excessive hunting. The rest of her story, is it not written in her obituary below?

MAGGIE, FIVE YEARS OLD

This March she arrived
And left in September,
Little hunting girl,
Black Labrador.
She liked the breeze
At the door,
Took naps
In the morning sun,
And loved to run.
Muscular, trim,
She liked to swim
In our creek.
Shiny fur, brown eyes,
She was catching mice.
In her way she talked.
On leash she walked
By Heidi's hand.
She loved this land,
Room to roam.
Greetings at home
When I came from work.

She wasn't sick,
Not very far
When hit by a car.
She liked us all,
Died second day of fall,
Buried the same night
Under star light
Bright.
Tender and tough,
Loved you and me.
That's good enough
For lasting memory.

ONE DAY AT A TIME[28]

Do not worry about tomorrow for tomorrow will worry about itself.
Each day has enough trouble of its own.

Matthew 6:34

During the fall of the year before the captain became a cadet, he was invited to spend a day and a night at West Point. In the morning was a presentation about life in the military academy. An enthusiastic female "Firsty" [senior], one of the twenty-five percent of competitive athletes in the Corps of Cadets, talked about her involvement, assignments, schedule, and extramural activity (pistol shooting). Then followed a question and answer period. The most relevant question was asked by the future captain: "How are you going to handle all that stress?" At this moment a sympathetic advisor asked to give the answer and said, "You take one day at a time. The whole series of assignments may overwhelm you, but you don't have to finish them all at once." This was the best advice I have ever heard, useful not only for future military leaders. It was fitting advice for all situations, as life so often confronts us with seemingly overwhelming challenges and crises. "Don't worry about tomorrow. Each day has enough trouble of its own." Just as we do not devour our food in one swallow, but chew it bite-size, so we are also to take our duties

---

28. "With Love to Mike & Sandy, Dad, 7-27-95"

one at time, controlled, effective, efficient. Even life we have received by an installment plan, one day at a time, with restful sleep in between, in order to "forget and sleep over the preceding day's trouble," as Matthias Claudius suggested in an old German evening song.

The advice of "One day at a time" can be further scrutinized by taking just one hour at a time. In such focus, time and duty intermesh amazingly well. There is, of course, an art of effective and decisive living, which can be learned and refined by self-discipline, organization, and practice, but may also be ignored and then possibly cause harm. Can packing so much activity into one day lead to wrong decisions? Yes, but an orderly process makes right decisions more likely than a wandering, idle approach to life. Taking one task and one day at a time become mandatory practices for handling professional pressure. Beyond our work, the advice applies to basic life itself including, emotions, suffering, and even tragedy.

Suicide in a family is probably one of the hardest tragedies to cope with as friends sadly experienced. A church meeting with special invitation convened to find a helpful answer in this case. There were laymen and clergy, but nobody could explain the tragedy, because basically there is no explanation. I suggested, "Bob, take one day at a time" and we adjourned. In the car on the way home, he said in parting, "So, take one day at a time?" That was the beginning of hope. It still took a lot of healing (one day at a time), and counseling, but from then on full restoration was in progress.

A GOOD LAUGH

"A cheerful heart is good medicine."

—*Proverbs 17:22*

"Even in laughter the heart may ache."

—*Proverbs 14:13*

In the late eighteen and early nineteen hundreds, our family led a simple, industrious life on a small farm, and did not forget to enjoy life through laughter. Since there was no electric light, they used petroleum lamps during the long fall and winter evenings. The women made down for feather beds from goose feathers, while grandpa told them stories. These included some special effects like sudden clapping of hands, when everybody woke up from the monotony of the chore to a hearty laugh. My father was a good storyteller, too. He used to conclude some stories by saying, "Everything has one end, only a sausage has two." He and his company also enjoyed practical jokes. One time he gave his daughters' friend a cactus, which was actually a look-alike, small cucumber stuck upright into a flowerpot. "You should always water it," he advised, which she did until the cucumber's rotten state gave its true nature away. Thus, jokes and laughter have run in the family. I'll never forget that we sang at the stairs to the house as a mixed trio, our Husky dog, our son and I, three dissonant voices raised toward the sky. Admittedly, the dog displayed most musical talent and soul. Our act was concluded by sneezing, first by the son, then by his dog, a truly hilarious performance.

We all have practiced and appreciated humorous speech and clean jokes, short and wordy. Two fleas left a theater. "Do we hop home, or shall we take a dog?" Or we laughed about a group of husbands. They came to the gate of heaven to stand in either of two lines; one for those dominated by their wives on earth, the other one for not dominated husbands. Only one stood there. "How did you manage such an independent life on earth?" the majority asked. "My wife told me to stand here," was the meek answer. Or we laughed about our daughter's observation in the state of Oklahoma, where rolls of hay were outlawed, because cows should have a square meal.

There is a subtle difference between jokes and humor. Something said or done to provoke laughter is a joke, but it may not be humor. Humor is an attitude of the heart, our inner being, something that is appreciated as comical. Jokes basically appeal to the mind, while the joker or his laughing audience may actually lack a sense of humor. The intellectual quality of a joke has to do with word plays, contradiction, paradox, mix-up, the shaking up of terms or pictures. An involuntary response may provoke laughter, too, likewise an instant rebuttal. Jokes need an audience and may share elements of a riddle, when they provoke the search for a hidden point. In contrast, a sense of humor requires the traits of freedom and distance. An ideologue is incapable of humor, because he sees only his side of an issue. Although the twentieth century's vicious dictators lacked a sense of humor, they could still joke and laugh, as verified by reports about Hitler and Stalin. At the other extreme is the comical and tragic effort of someone attempting a powerless verbal revenge. A true sense of humor goes together with inner sovereignty and a position above the circumstances. This will go a long way, but even such humor has its limitations, namely in crisis cases, where only faith will work.

Why do we laugh? People have written books about it. Psychologists have probed the issue, since a sense of humor or the lack of it may shed light into a person's psyche. But such rationalizations are no longer funny. The Roman orator Cicero remarked that a person of some education could write with humor about any subject, except about humor.

Many people claim to have a sense of humor. Presumably they base their claim on liking jokes, having fun, or laughing about someone else. I have observed that many of them wince and whine when someone else pokes fun at them. Obviously, they had put themselves on a pedestal. To me a sense of humor means to be able to laugh heartily about myself. Interestingly, the less seriously I took myself, the more seriously I considered others. I was not born with this refined sense of humor, but now I have practiced it for several decades. Ever since I have laughed a most liberating laughter.[29]

---

29. I have never met a person with a more wholesome, infectious laugh than my father. His laughter caused sympathetic detonations of joy.

TYME AND TYDE

"You are my God. My times are in your hands."

—Psalm 31:14-15

The inscription on the old clock read "Tyme and Tyde never end." If I ever had wanted to get into antique clocks, this one would have aroused a collector's special interest, this handsome, grey metal box with Roman numerals and a thought-provoking message. Our friend's father, a fatherly friend to us, had bought it in London at the end of the eighteen hundreds, when he visited Britain as a young engineer. The clock was already old. Now, at the end of the nineteen hundreds, it was visibly positioned on his son's mantelpiece and still working. His son was not. He was paralyzed. My brothers were his friends, and I was a friend. Our friend [Ernst Brockhaus] was not always paralyzed. We used to swim together. I was then barely tolerated by those big boys when they frolicked in the pool and demonstrated their diving skills. Now we talked, and I sensed the tides come and go with time, repeating themselves without end, as the earth's oceans and its moon interacted in mechanical order. We did not feel gravity's tug, but heard the ticking of the clock.

Before the middle of the century, the most unnecessary war was provoked. All wars seem unnecessary, but some have followed at least a measure of logic or defensive justification. This one featured "heroism" in lieu of common sense, with total disregard for the rest of the world, for the basics at logistics, and for the technological, industrial, economical potential of the United States. Since the majority of any nation does not consist of heroes, the greatest gamble of the century was also silly. Yet millions were sucked into it, including our friend, his brother, and friends. Mother prayed that her sons would not be crippled in the war, and her prayer was heard. By grace, they and our friend's brother were not crippled. It was hard grace, however, since they did not come back either. Our friend did, young, newly married, shot through his head, paralyzed, some upper body functions left intact.

It was then when we became friends. I pushed his wheelchair to church and back for miles, up and down a long hill, visited, talked, laughed. One time he laughingly asked me why I was moaning. He had a good laugh. We were late. With his wife and their little son, he moved into the countryside. Occasionally I would still visit and push him around a lake. This went on for years, until I would not only be a friend, but also an emigrant. I'll never forget how his face briefly trembled when I said goodbye. There were not too many people visiting or remembering him. Everybody was dancing around the golden calf. Did I not also pursue my personal happiness in family and career when I moved far away? Often, I would think of him. Sporadically, I would still write, call, visit once, while he lived his lonely life with his wife, often smiling, his clear, blue eyes keenly open toward those who cared.

On May 2, in the air between Chicago and San Francisco, I suddenly had to think of my friend. Quickly I prayed. Although already at high altitude, one could still get much closer to heaven. In the middle of July, I spent just a week in Glasgow, London, and Düsseldorf, from where I called. "Your friend is no more; he died on May the second, seventy-nine years old." Unwinding from deep mourning and loneliness, his wife relived in minute details for half an hour his last weeks, how they reaffirmed their faith, recited Psalms, and shared their experience of God as a friend. "Isn't this true? Yes, this is true." I could only listen to learn how he confidently lived and died. Not every disabled person is blessed with a loving spouse. Not every widow can look back on a noble life of unselfish service.

I sensed the coming of the tide. A gentle wave washed his long suffering away. Eventually, high tide will wash over our sandcastles, too, when they have served their purpose. The earth and the moon still interact, stern and steadily followed by ocean tides. We hear the waves' soothing refrain on the beaches. On our watch, time and tide never end. God's love never ceases.

TYME AND TYDE

The old clock moved its hand:
Tyme and tyde never end.
Century old in eighty-seven,
It belonged to my friend,
Who is now in heaven.

The clock was working,
While he was not.
Young, newly married,
He was shot,
His paralyzed life
Shared by his wife.

For years I went
To be his friend,
Pushed his wheel-chair
Once here, once there,
But on one day
Moved far away.

Through days and nights,
Tides followed tides:
Sea-moon interaction
Without our detection

Of gravity's tug.
Still ticked the clock.

On the second of May –
Impelled to pray
For my friend far away –
Came the end of his life,
As told by his wife:
"Talked of God as a friend."
Then the clock moved its hand.

Tides' steady display,
Day after day,
Waves' soothing refrain:
His freedom's gain.
Time and tide never end
On our watch, my friend.

HWR
8/30/95

THE ACCIDENT

"The Lord will protect him and preserve his life."

—Psalm 41:2

It was a one-car plus driver accident. No other vehicle or person was involved. It happened in the early evening on January twenty-fourth, on the way home from work. Wet snow had fallen that afternoon, as I was slowly descending the lonely road through the woods again, in four-wheel drive at about fifteen miles per hour. Suddenly my Bronco [II] was sliding to the left, left front end first, got into the left ditch, tipped onto its right side on the road, then completely rolled over toward the right side of the road, where it came to rest in a slanted position of about forty-five degrees, in original driving direction, its left wheels deep in the right ditch, its right wheels somewhat above the ditch, the engine still running. I turned it off, got out of my seatbelt and out of the left door, and collected several items thrown onto the road. Even though it sounds unlikely, I later succeeded to back the badly damaged vehicle in four-wheel drive out of the ditch and drove it home, personally without pain or injury. The good Lord had protected me, while the Bronco was totaled.

We are always surrounded by dangers, often without knowing. Accidents can happen at home, at work, anywhere. People may come out of their driveways too quickly, pass recklessly on the road, or stop suddenly.

There are safe and unsafe practices. It makes sense to slow down and to spend a few minutes to think a new job through, how it might affect others and oneself. A tall ladder could be fastened to avoid its sliding away. Haste not only makes waste, it can also injure or kill. So can lack of concentration or observation. Some people are notoriously accident-prone. A neighbor in Germany always seemed to walk absent-mindedly, or was riding his bike that way. Sadly, one time too often, he overlooked a streetcar and was killed.

Many, perhaps most accidents are avoidable, including the one described above, for instance, by not choosing that road on that evening, or by driving a not so top-heavy vehicle. But, taking human nature and circumstances into consideration, some accidents are apt to happen. If something is conceivable, it is usually also possible and may find its way into reality.

How then can we live safer lives? "Be very careful how you live." That takes thought and the right attitude toward life and others. Beyond patience and defensive measures, it also takes a guardian angel. I know that I was accompanied by a very skillful one who softened my landing after flip-flopping from one ditch to the other, in slow motion at fifteen miles per hour. Of course, one should never drive faster than a guardian angel can fly.

THE LUNCH BREAK

"So in everything, do to others what you would have them do to you."

—Matthew 7:12

Friedhof is the German word for cemetery, with the meaning "place of peace." How many millions in all the ages went through their lives full of anxiety, until at least their bodies came to rest in peace? Many cemeteries enhance their peaceful setting by fine landscaping. Always attracted by natural scenery, I have liked to visit cemeteries. Occasionally they have also provided history lessons or opportunities for reflection and respect. Before I went to school in my hometown, a certain Mr. Krombach, then in his seventies, used to pick me up to accompany him to the graves of his loved ones. I remember that he took care of little red flowers there and explained that the dead appreciate this attention. It was just a gesture of love or memory, and possibly of self-respect. Thus, early on, I was initiated to a natural attitude about these quiet, often shunned places.

During my time in Chicagoland, I found extensive cemeteries just a few miles west of the city. One was much congested by stone monuments and reflected tremendous waste, actually more death than the dead themselves. I could sense a metropolitan march by the tens of thousands into such habitat for several decades. Another cemetery featured a pleasant, park-like setting. Located near my place of work, it invited a stroll and relaxation during my lunch break. There and then I made some interesting observations, of which I'll share just two. By necessity, death is associated with merchants of death. I'm not talking about merchants of arms, just about the funeral business in a wide sense. It is unfortunate for the consumer that both businesses are very lucrative. Somewhat hilly, the cemetery offered good vantage points. So, I saw a large station wagon pulling up at a dumping place for old wreaths and wilted flowers. Two ladies got out and began sorting things. First, I thought that they were discarding objects, but I noticed soon that it was the other way around. They selected artificial wreaths, flowers, and ornaments for recycling. Now, generally I am all in favor of recycling, but what about an expensive wreath for your loved one that had already served for decoration or affection at another funeral? Waste not, want not? Yankee ingenuity to make a buck, or to overcome competitive pressure? Or was it a most tasteless case of greed? The dead didn't mind. After all, they had learned to forgive by now, if they had not practiced it during life.

The other observation perturbed me more. A funeral was in progress on a sunny spring day. The coffin was already put into the ground. Reddish yellow clay was piled up beside the open grave. A backhoe with driver waited nearby, replacing old-fashioned grave digging. The mourners were middle-age ladies in colorful dresses, chatting and apparently remembering a fellow sister for an extended time, a thoughtful picture that initiated my own reflections. Suddenly, the heavy equipment roared into motion. A few aimed movements and the clay was transferred into the hole; the grave was leveled. Within minutes the scene resembled a small building site of widely scratched soil. Now, not only the deceased person was gone, the grave was gone, too. The ladies had scattered like chickens, but now came back to look for the grave in vain. At no other time have I experienced such brutality. Yes, it was noontime, and the driver wanted to have a lunch break, too. What a contrast to Mr. Krombach's tenderness. Did it matter? It mattered to me, a stranger to all involved, below the ground and above.

FRIENDSHIP IN FALL

Gently molded,
Downward folded
Woodland hills:
A harvested field
Within their realm,
A protective shield
Of maple and elm.

The morning mist
Was slowly rising
Through azure sky
And landscape flooding
Light from up high,
A majestic way
To color this day.

In harmony heard
A soft-spoken bird,
Picked its breakfast seed
Among deep-red leaves,
Picture-perfect deed,
Heart-felt tune in all:
God's friendship in fall.

Horst Rauhut
9-24-95

FALL FUNERAL

"Where, o death, is your victory?"

—I Corinthians 15:55

He was a special resident in our valley, Vernon Jordan, old bachelor and veteran. Decades ago he served as school teacher in our township. He also took care of his parents' little plot of land, and then of his parents until they died. An active member of the Community Church, he painted its steeple white already in his seventies. Slowly he drove through the valley in his very old car, went to bed with the birds, and awoke early. Thus, he hardly used any electricity. Yet he amended his minimal means and frugality with generous giving to his church. Vernon was such an orderly, organized, helpful man of high standards. Not surprisingly, many people liked him, and his extended family loved him. So, they wished him a long life, and the good Lord granted their desire, up to a point. Then our old friend died.

I'm glad that I went to his funeral, because it turned out to be a happy and special event. The funeral was around noon, but I still had to take some time off from work. While driving to the country cemetery in bright sunshine, I was surrounded by an abundance of fall colors. Actually, I became fully immersed in the bright red and gold tones of our maple trees, in harmonious contrast with the dark green distribution of pines and firs, under a perfectly blue sky. Thus, I arrived at the gravesite in an unusually joyful mood, still on time before the service began. There were mostly elderly folks by the elevated casket, which was to receive warm, late rays from a gracious nature, together with sincere blessings from a young preacher. He rightfully praised and acknowledged Vernon's outreach and contributions to others, prayed, and soon closed his service. However, nobody wanted to leave. The environment was just too inviting, the separation from our old friend too soon. People chatted, reminisced, and visited with old acquaintances. Everybody appeared joyful; well, almost everybody. Vernon's cousin, with a failing heart, did not feel well during the funeral; he was also the next of us to follow. We must be mindful of a balanced view and not overlook the fact that death is an irreversible transition in our lives. Then one broadly smiling lady expressed the desire to see Vernon one more time, and several others immediately concurred. So the casket was partially opened for a last goodbye, accompanied by happy expressions. It occurred to me that Vernon Jordan himself took the opportunity for one more peek into our beautifully created world, while he resided already in the bliss and perfection of a superior kingdom. "Where, o death, is your sting?" How marvelous is autumn, the dying season, with its crescendo of colorful flowers and leaves, preceding multiple lives' relief from activity into a quiet, dormant state of joyful expectation.

HONKING HIGH

The wide valley fills
With blooming golden rod.
Brightly painted hills
Overlook my winding path
Near soft-green alfalfa
And half-harvested corn,
Silk corn in seclusion.

Faintly I hear you honk,
High in the blue sky,
Beyond wooded vegetation,
And there you all fly
In a great V-formation,
Flying south by the sun
In the southeastern sky.

Against sun's bright light
I cover my eyes, but watch
Your marvelous flight
And listen, as I hear much
Happy honking all the way.
Although flying all night,
You'll still travel today.

Here is corn, here is water,
But you plan to feed much later.
Stretched-out neck,
And eyes on focus,
Don't look back,

While you must leave us,
Honking all the way.

Three of you now change position,
Flying forward in the Vee,
Now rejoin the V-formation,
There where you prefer to be.
While your branch moves like a whip,
All of you honk extra loud
And straighten out.

Farewell, long-distance fliers,
Create and use your wake.
Fly over us and by us,
Fly, reach a southern lake.
Farewell, Canadian geese,
I realize you cannot sing,
Just honk when you return in spring.

WHEN PARENTS PASS

Precious in the sight of the Lord is the death of his saints.

— Psalm 116:15

Nothing really prepares you for the loss of your parents, or any loved-one for that matter. Our mental frame is such that our parent's mortality seems to sneak up on us despite the obvious reality that we grow old and die; life and death are inextricably linked as the introduction highlights. Unknown to us, Dad was struggling with cancer. He had been hospitalized a few times for health complications and an injury, but Dad had kept the extent of his cancer from us. While stationed in Georgia in October 2011, I received my sister's call that Dad was not well, had been hospitalized, and ultimately was coming home for hospice care. I drove home immediately, arriving the day he came home. During the week I was able to spend with my Dad before returning to Georgia to collect Sandy and our children, he shared many happy memories and gave instructions and advice. He deteriorated quickly, passing on November 2nd, 2011. His funeral was remarkable for the testimonies people gave; to his character, charity, gentle spirit, and humility. My sisters and I shared our memories. I chose to share a poem he had written for his mother, "A Lady of Faith."

We were blessed with Mom's continued presence in our lives for six and a half additional years. Mom too showed immense grace, thankfulness, and love as we spent the last few days of her life together. She passed early on Sunday morning, the 6th of May 2018. Her funeral too was marked by love. We miss them both so very much. On the occasion of Mom's passing, I wrote the following poem, inspired by my Dad's poem for his own mother and read at my Mom's funeral, May 12, 2018:

ANOTHER "LADY OF FAITH"

She endured early trials that shaped her life.
She saw death and destruction,
yet grew new and alive.
She met a young man, familiar and shy,
with similar hardships, yet just as alive.

Their love brought new life into this world,
and an adventure across a vast ocean sea.
A new country, an odd language,
and more life came to be.

Love of God and family constant,
her faith in the Name dutifully hallowed.

She supported her love and moved yet again,
learning new ways of living, without and within.
She connected to community, church and her ministry,
sharing love and good news.
She served others first; the elderly and young,
women and men, neighbors all.
She grew older, prayed more, shared her love;
losing her soul mate but shining still.
She left us Sunday morning,
finally at peace, after a life of hardship and joy.

She was more than a minister and friend.
She was my Mom.

She read to me and sang to me of God's love and grace;
She cared for me and showed me His un-seeable face.
She prayed for me as I grew older and fought in a dangerous place.

She loved my wife and children, and shared in all their trials.
She never stopped praying, not even for a while.
She talked with me daily, until her final hours, sharing her love for us all.

I share the same sentiment for my Mom that my Dad held for his:
"Her inner strength and example persuaded me to follow her path of trust."

Another Notable Lady of Faith.

EPILOGUE

"He has told you, O man, what is good; and what does the LORD require of you but to do justice, and to love kindness, and to walk humbly with your God?"

— *Micah 6:8*

When I reflect on our parents' lives, I am struck by their justice, mercy, and faithfulness, shaped by generations of unique trials. It is remarkable to note that our parent's audio matched their video. They were not perfect, but they endeavored to live the values they espoused and provide an example still. Beyond their selfless example, I am also overwhelmed by our good fortune in benefitting from their tests and receiving special gifts; an unwarranted legacy of faith, love, and sacrifice. Regrettably, far too many people have not experienced, as we have, a legacy of love and freedom. For many, navigating life has become so complicated and burdensome that they find themselves in servitude rather than free.[30] Life still requires choice and action as each generation decides for itself what it will do with what it has been presented. Like my parents, I imperfectly pursue the answer I found and for which I find no substitute; do justice, love kindness, and walk humbly with my God.

There's another aspect of our parents' story that bears further contem-

---

30. For an interesting exploration of freedom, life's navigability, and nudges, see Cass R. Sunstein's, On Freedom, Princeton University Press, 2019.

plation. Reflecting and storytelling help make the unknowable recognizable. Storytelling has always been important. In no small measure the deeds described by my parents, through the oral stories I grew up listening to, led me to a lifetime of service in our United States Army. Young men from this same Army liberated my parents in 1945 and showed incredible compassion to two unknown children, in two different towns, and in the midst of life-ending chaos. Unknown U.S. Department of State employees helped my family immigrate and continue freedom's journey, the same Department with which I've been fortunate to work closely the last five years as we advanced U.S. interests. I have been blessed to serve with incredibly gifted and talented civil servants and soldiers, men and women of immense character, virtue, and selflessness. On the most granular level, there was no way for Burt Marsh, Charles Faulconer, or their comrades to know that how they conducted themselves, the example they set, would have a direct impact on my decision to serve that same Army on other battlefields sixty years later. Neither could they know that along with Command Sergeants Major Del Byers, Jeremiah Inman, Jason Silsby, and Bobby Gallardo, I would share my family story to convey to our soldiers our gratitude for their service and to never underestimate the impact they may have on others; to do either justice or show mercy to those to whom each was due. So, please be encouraged. Reflect, recognize, and tell your story; live your purpose in deeds, not just words.

August 2018
Charles Faulconer, Mike Rauhut, and Burt Marsh
80th Infantry Division Reunion

August 2017
Celebrating Magdalena Rauhut's 86th Birthday

Finally, faithfulness bears fruit. The photo above, taken at our Mother's 85th birthday, is just a snap shot in time of our parent's progeny. As is clear from the stories herein, she and my Dad impacted lives far beyond our immediate family. We hope you have benefitted or been touched in a meaningful way by our parent's story, and we look forward to watching, hearing, or reading yours. Thank you.

APPENDIX A

REMARKS BY AMBASSADOR
SAMANTHA POWER

January 13, 2017
Ambassador Samantha Power and Colonel Mike Rauhut
United States Mission to the United Nations

Remarks by Ambassador Samantha Power on Welcoming New American Citizens and Receiving the "Outstanding American by Choice" Award[31] from the U.S. Citizenship and Immigration Services, November 15, 2016

United States Mission to the United Nations
Office of Press and Public Diplomacy
799 United Nations Plaza
New York, NY 10017
(212) 415-4050
http://usun.state.gov

As Delivered   November 15, 2016

It is such an honor to be here, and I thank you so much for choosing me for the award, especially because it gives me the chance to be a part of the ceremony for these 15 new Americans. I'd like to start my remarks just with a few stories.

Akram Razzouk was a university student in Beirut when Lebanon's brutal civil war broke out. It was not long before the army and militia were going door to door, enlisting every able-bodied man and boy to fight. Akram dreamed of studying medicine, and with his professors' encouragement, he applied for a visa to go to the United States. He never expected to get one, but he did, together with a spot at a medical school in California. Akram left Beirut carrying a few hundred dollars, two pairs of pants, and a few shirts. He was 19 years old. Two days after he arrived in the United States of America, soldiers showed up at his family's home to conscript him. It was 1973.

In 1952, Chock Wai Wong was 15 years old, in Taishan, Chi-

---

31. Used with permission of Ambassador Power, email and phone confirmation, March 2018.

na, when he heard that the Communist Party was coming to register new members in his village. Not wanting to be there when they showed up, he fled to Hong Kong, where he spent most of his family's savings on a boat ticket to America. When he arrived, he and the other Chinese passengers aboard were quarantined on Angel's Island off the coast of San Francisco. Eventually allowed to come ashore, he made his way to Cedar Rapids, Iowa, where he started working in a Chinese restaurant run by his relatives. He eventually returned briefly to Hong Kong to marry, before going back to Iowa, where he took on every shift he could in the restaurant—pinching pennies so he could bring his wife and newborn daughter to America.

In April 1945, the U.S. army liberated the German town of Halberstadt from the Nazis. American soldiers went house to house, making sure that there were no Nazi soldiers hiding inside. One door was answered by a 12-year-old named Horst Rauhut. Horst had lost four members of his immediate family in the war—two brothers, who died fighting on the eastern front; a sister killed in an artillery strike; and his father, a firefighter, who was killed in an air raid. When Horst saw the U.S. soldiers on the doorstep, he figured they had come for revenge. But the Americans were respectful and generous, even sharing some of their food with him—something he never forgot. After the war, Horst became a chemist and married a girl from a neighboring town that had also been liberated by Americans. As they started a family of their own, they watched the Berlin Wall go up and saw tensions rise again in their country. Fearful that their children might have to suffer through a war as they had when they were younger, they applied to come to the United States. In 1964, Horst, his wife, and their two young daughters boarded a flight to Washington, D.C.

Here's my last story. In 1901, Joseph Steinberg left the shtetl in Kyiv, Ukraine. The Jewish residents there were routinely the target of mob attacks called pogroms. He set out for America to build a new life for his family. He left behind a pregnant wife and two children, and made the journey to New York, where he built a wooden pushcart on wheels, from which he sold eyeglasses. Customers would simply try on pairs until they found one—it's impossible—until they found one pair of eyeglasses that could help them see. It took Joseph three years to sell enough glasses to send for his family—including his youngest son, Morris, who he had never met. Picking his family up at Ellis Island, Joseph brought the family to their new home. It was in a tenement building on Rivington Street, just a few blocks away from where we are today.

These are the stories of just four individuals who—like those of you who have become citizens here today—made a journey to become citizens of the United States. There are millions of stories like them. There are 15—I guarantee you—sitting right here. And taken together, these stories are the threads that weave together the rich and intricate fabric of our nation. A nation that is now your nation, and in which your thread—which runs back through your ancestors—will now be a unique part.

Now, because I could have told a lot of stories, you might be wondering, 'Why those four stories?' Well, I picked these stories because these are the families of four of the many people who now serve with me in the U.S. government at the U.S. Mission to the United Nations, helping represent our nation—the United States—to the world.

Remember Akram Razzouk—whose story I started with—Akram who fled Lebanon's civil war to come here to study medicine in California? His daughter Kelly is a U.S. career civil servant and a leading human rights expert at the U.S. Mission.

The baby daughter whom Chock Wai Wong worked endless

restaurant shifts in Cedar Rapids, Iowa, to bring here from China was named Kam. She's been serving in the State Department for 25 years—the last two years with me here in New York.

Horst Rauhut—the 12-year-old whose town was liberated by American soldiers during the Second World War—eventually came to America, where he and his wife had their third child. That boy, Mike, went on to study at West Point, and is now our highest-ranking military officer at the U.S. Mission to the UN.

And Joseph Steinberg, who sold eyeglasses on the streets around this museum to get his family out of the shtetl, is the great-grandfather of one of my closest advisors, Nik Steinberg.

Before I lose it further [laughter], let me ask three of the individuals I just named—Kam, Mike, and Nik—to stand up. They're here with us. I couldn't be more honored to get to work with these amazing public servants every day.

Thirty-seven years ago, as well, my family also came to this country as immigrants from Dublin, Ireland. I was nine when my mother, my younger brother, and I landed in Pittsburgh. I remember thinking that I had never seen a bigger or fancier place in my life. Fourteen years later, in a courthouse in Brooklyn—having studied for that test—having been terrified about that test [laughter]—I became a U.S. citizen. And for the last three years, I—an immigrant—have had the privilege of sitting behind the placard that says United States of America at the United Nations.

Now, you may think that I have picked exceptional stories of people who work with me at the U.S. Mission to the UN, but as we heard here, every U.S. government agency is made up of people whose families made similarly remarkable journeys. And it is not just the U.S. government that looks like this. It is the teachers who educate our children. It is the doctors and the nurses who take care of our sick. It is the workers who staff our businesses—from factories to high tech. Everywhere you look, this is what America looks like. You are what America looks like. And as much as any other quality, this is what makes this country so exceptional.

Today, you, too, have become citizens of this nation—at a pretty tumultuous time, as you may have read in the newspapers [laughter]. For some of you, this may be a day of mixed emotions. I suspect many of you were drawn to this country not only because of the opportunities it offers—but also because of the principles that it stands for and strives to live up to. A nation built on the values of freedom and justice, and the idea that all citizens have the right to be treated equally, and with dignity.

And yet we have just come through an election campaign in which some of these very principles have been called into question. We've heard politicians, public figures, and citizens call for people to be treated differently because of what they believe or because of where they were born. We've heard immigrants blamed for many of our country's problems.

Sadly, this is far from the first time. We are a nation of immigrants, but for as long as this amazing country has existed, people have been harkening back to a mythical golden era, before families like yours or mine got here. It never seems to matter to those people that their own parents or their own grandparents were often on the receiving end of similar discrimination when they first arrived in this country.

But even if we know deep down that such intolerance is as old as the nation itself—as every nation—it doesn't make it hurt any less when we experience it. And it doesn't make us any less concerned or any less afraid when we see a spike in reported hate crimes as we have in just the last week.

I imagine that this most recent stretch may have led some of you to ask whether this is the America that you thought you were joining. It may even have led a few of you to reconsider whether you wanted to become U.S. citizens. Yet a week after such a divisive election, here you are, taking this critical, beautiful step.

Since I have a couple decades' head start on you, I hope you will allow me to offer just a few parting thoughts on what it means to become an American—and just as important, what it does not mean.

You may hear some people say that—in order to become real Americans—you need to forget where you came from, or leave behind the history that brought you to this moment. Cover up your accent. Change the way you dress. Stick to neighborhoods where immigrants like you live. Please don't listen to those voices. Joining a new nation does not mean you have to leave behind the one you came from or what it taught you.

Every one of those individuals whose histories I shared at the outset here today is a better citizen and a better public servant because of the values that their immigrant families brought with them from other places.

Kelly Razzouk fights harder for the freedom of political prisoners because she knows her father may well have been one of them, had he been unable to leave Lebanon. Kam Wong treats every single individual who walks through the doors of the U.S. Mission to the UN with decency—regardless of who they are or where they're from—in part because she remembers how much it meant to her Chinese-speaking mother when—shortly after arriving in Iowa—a neighbor knocked on her door and offered to teach the family English. Nik Steinberg is driven to work harder on behalf of refugees fleeing violence and persecution because he knows what would have happened to his relatives if no country had taken them in. And Mike Rauhut is an even better military leader because he carries with him the indelible lessons of his parents' experience — of being liberated by soldiers who treated them with dignity and compassion.

The same goes for me. The qualities I rely most on as a diplomat and in my most important job, as a mother of two small children, are ones I learned from my mother and father, both of whom are Irish immigrants. My father's sitting here with us today. [Applause.] All of this history is what makes our citizens and our nation so exceptional. Why would we ever want to give that up? So don't listen to those who say you have to choose between being a proud American and a proud immigrant. You can be both. You must be both.

Of course, even as you are careful not to give up a sense of where you've come from, you mustn't let that be the only thing that defines you. Of course you have your roots. Your family. Your faith. The parts of you that — no matter where you go — will always feel like home. But while those roots will always anchor you in the ground, they are also what allow you to reach to the sky — if only you let them. In this amazing city of ours, you have a unique opportunity to engage with people who are so different from you — just in your little cohort here today. Engage them. Get to know them. You'll be surprised how much you can learn from them — and, of course, they from you.

I believe that one of the reasons our nation feels so divided of late is because this mingling, this engagement isn't happening nearly enough — not just among immigrants, but all Americans. It's easier to fear others if we never have a chance to talk with them. When we get to know them, we're often surprised to discover that beneath all the parts on the outside that appear so different, there is so much on the inside that is the same. And the more we learn to see ourselves in our fellow citizens, and walk around in their shoes, the less it becomes us and them, and the more it becomes just us.

Now, you may also hear some people say that, because you haven't been here as long, you somehow deserve less of a say in shaping our nation. Nonsense. As of today, America is as much your county as it is any other citizen's country. That is your right. But that right—like all the others that are now yours—comes with a profound and enduring responsibility.

And on that responsibility, I would like to close with a brief story—a familiar story some of you may have even learned in studying American history for your citizenship exam, and a story that feels particularly relevant in these times. In 1787—a long time ago—delegates from 12 of the United States' 13 colonies gathered in Philadelphia's State House with the aim of reforming their government. They spent more than four months wrangling over the document that would eventually become our nation's Constitution. When the news spread that they had finally reached an agreement, citizens rushed to the State House to learn what had happened. As one delegate, Benjamin Franklin, walked out of the building, a woman stopped him and asked, "Well, Doctor, what have we got—a republic or a monarchy?" Franklin quickly replied: "A republic, if you can keep it." A republic, if you can keep it.

Now, Franklin was a founding father. Few had done more to define the principles at the heart of our then-young nation—ones he felt the Constitution was "near to perfection" in reflecting. But even then—even a founding father, even Franklin—recognized that whether the United States lived up to those ideals and succeeded as a nation would not be determined by any document, or even any government, but rather rested in the hands of America's citizens. Not by words on a page, but by the actions of real people.

A republic, if you can keep it. A republic, if we can keep it. We, citizens.

In a moment, I'm going to be asking you to place your hand

on your heart and pledge allegiance to our republic. As you do, remember where you came from, and draw strength from it. Don't let anyone tell you that because you are a new citizen, you are a second-class citizen. We only have one class of citizens here in America.

And remember that allegiance is about much more than just abiding by a system of laws. Today, you are sworn into what the great Supreme Court Justice Louis Brandeis once called the most important office in our land—that of private citizen. The office of private citizen carries with it an awesome responsibility and an unparalleled privilege of being one of the individuals empowered to keep our republic strong. The fate of our nation, your nation—and everything it stands for—has and always will depend on it. Depend on us. We trust that you are up to the task, and we welcome you to this country with open arms.

Now, as your first act as American citizens, I would ask that you please rise and join me in the Pledge of Allegiance.

I pledge allegiance to the Flag of the United States of America and to the Republic for which it stands, one nation, under God, indivisible, with liberty and justice for all.

Thank you so much, and congratulations!

APPENDIX B
HONOR ROLL

319TH INFANTRY, 329TH INFANTRY, AND
1ST BATTALION, 22ND INFANTRY REGIMENTS

319ᵀᴴ INFANTRY REGIMENT, 80TH INFANTRY DIVISION
"Losses in Action, Officers and Men"[32]
vic Glauchau, Germany
[Liberated Magdalena Rauhut (Winkel)]

14-15 APRIL 1945

Private First Class	Ronald Pagliari	KIA	Co G	14 April 1945
Private First Class	Edward Walker	KIA	Co G	14 April 1945
Staff Sergeant	Salvatore Sargente	WIA/DOW	Co G	14 April 1945
Corporal	Roy Schlesinger	WIA	Co H	14 April 1945
Private First Class	Andrew Tuesday	WIA	Co H	14 April 1945
Private First Class	Jose E. Candelaria	WIA	Co G	14 April 1945
Private First Class	Duward A. Peterson	WIA	Co G	14 April 1945
Sergeant	Byron E. Sparks	WIA	Co G	14 April 1945
Private	Adolf W. Paul	WIA	Co G	14 April 1945
Private	Ray F. Miller	WIA	Co G	14 April 1945
Private	Robert M. Thomas	WIA	Co G	14 April 1945
Private First Class	William E. Ryan	WIA	Co G	14 April 1945
Private	Willis Geehring	WIA	Co G	14 April 1945
Second Lieutenant	James W. Clark	WIA	Co I	14 April 1945
Staff Sergeant	Henry D. Turberville	WIA	Co G	14 April 1945
Technician Fourth Grade	Carmine G. Liotti	KIA	Medical Det.	15 April 1945
Technician Fifth Grade	John A. Carbin	KIA	Medical Det.	15 April 1945
Sergeant	Merrill O. Carner	KIA	Co F	15 April 1945

32. 80th Division Digital Archives Project, "Headquarters 319th Infantry, Office of the Regimental Commander, APO 80, U.S. Army Unit History (For Month of April), Section IX: Losses in Action, Officers and Men" http://www.80thdivision.com/ UnitHistories/319thInfReg_UnitHistory_APR45-partial_1.pdf accessed 21 March 2018.

Private	Robert H. Quinn	KIA	Co F	15 April 1945
Second Lieutenant	Wynne B. Handy	KIA	Co G	15 April 1945
Staff Sergeant	Byron E. Sparks	DOW	Co G	15 April 1945
Corporal	John W. Boire	WIA/DOW	Medical Det.	15 April 1945
Private First Class	Harry W. Heiberger	WIA/DOW	Medical Det.	15 April 1945
Private First Class	George Pfeiffer	MIA	AT Co	15 April 1945
Sergeant	John O. Bauer	WIA	Co B	15 April 1945
Staff Sergeant	Ralph R. Passard	WIA	Co B	15 April 1945
Private	Kenneth L. LeClear	WIA	Medical Det.	15 April 1945
Private First Class	Mario D. Garza	WIA	Co F	15 April 1945
Private	Harold W. Siverd	WIA	Co F	15 April 1945
Corporal	Sydney Harzler	WIA	Co F	15 April 1945
Private	Clinton C. McCollum	WIA	Co F	15 April 1945
Staff Sergeant	Sylvester S. Snyder	WIA	Co F	15 April 1945
Private First Class	Ralph M. Brown	WIA	Co F	15 April 1945
Private First Class	Thomas J. Fitzsimmons	WIA	Co G	15 April 1945
Private First Class	Elvin D. French	WIA	Co G	15 April 1945

GLOSSARY

Pvt./Pfc.—Private (no insignia)/Private First Class (today abbreviated PFC)

Tec 4—Technician Fourth Grade (T/4.). Would be addressed as "Sergeant"; the rank no longer exists; modern rank equivalent would be a Sergeant (SGT).

S/Sgt—Staff Sergeant (today abbreviated SSG)

Tec 5—Technician Fifth Grade (T/5.). Would be addressed as "Corporal" or "Tech Corporal"; the rank no longer exists; modern rank equivalent would be a Specialist (SPC).

T/Sgt—Technical Sergeant (today a Sergeant First Class & abbreviated SFC)

AT — Anti-Tank

Det. — Detachment

2d Lt — Second Lieutenant (today abbreviated 2LT)

CO — Company

NMI — No Middle Initial

DOW — Died of Wounds

KIA — Killed in Action

SWA — Seriously Wounded in Action

LWA — Lightly Wounded in Action

MIA — Missing in Action

329TH INFANTRY REGIMENT (COMBAT TEAM 329), 83RD INFANTRY DIVISION

"Losses In Action"[33]

vic Halberstadt, Germany

[Liberated Horst Rauhut]

11 APRIL 1945

Private First Class	Herman H. Zinzel	KIA	11 April 1945
Sergeant	James/Joseph H. Glover*	MIA/KIA	11 April 1945
Staff Sergeant	John NMI Chepan	SWA	11 April 1945
Technical Sergeant	Samuel P. Stepanovich	LWA	11 April 1945
Private First Class	Henry W. Buckles	LWA	11 April 1945
Private First Class	Hildaige G. Savoie	LWA	11 April 1945
Private First Class	Paul L. Dunn	LWA	11 April 1945
Private First Class	Theodore J. Letterie	LWA	11 April 1945
Private First Class	John J. Seehorsch	LWA	11 April 1945
Technician Fifth Grade	Curtis P. Swihart	LWA	11 April 1945
First Sergeant	Ralph NMI Bailey	LWA	11 April 1945
Technical Sergeant	Harry L. Martin	LWA	11 April 1945
Private First Class	Orie E. Taylor, Jr.	LWA	11 April 1945

GLOSSARY

PFC—Private First Class

T/Sgt—Technical Sergeant (today a Sergeant First Class & abbreviated SFC)

S/Sgt—Staff Sergeant (today abbreviated SSG)

Tec 5—Technician Fifth Grade (T/5.) Would be addressed as "Corpo-

33 83rd Infantry Division Documents, 329th After Action Report April 1945, Section VIII, Losses In Action, pp 3-4, 6. https://83rdinfdivdocs.org/documents/329th/AAR/AAR_329_APR1945.pdf accessed 24 March 2018.

ral" or "Tech Corporal"; the rank no longer exists; modern rank equivalent would be a Specialist (SPC).

KIA — Killed in Action

SWA — Seriously Wounded in Action

LWA — Lightly Wounded in Action

MIA — Missing in Action

NMI — No Middle Initial

*Roster reflects an entry for "James H. Glover" MIA on 11 April and later "Joseph H. Glover" KIA on 11 April. Same serial number listed, so I presume a clerical error or update to earlier report of MIA.

1ST BATTALION, 22ND INFANTRY REGIMENT, 4TH INFANTRY DIVISION
Losses in Action
Iraq
2003-2004

First Lieutenant	Osbaldo Orozco	KIA	Co C	25 April 2003
Private	Jesse Halling	KIA	401st MP Co	6 June 2003
Private First Class	Analaura Esparza Gutierrez	KIA	Co A, 4th Fwd Spt Bn	1 October 2003
Specialist	James E. Powell	KIA	Co B	12 October 2003
Specialist	Donald L. Wheeler, Jr.	KIA	Co C	13 October 2003
Private First Class	Ervin Dervishi	KIA	Co B	24 January 2004
Corporal	Juan Cabral	WIA/KIA	Co A, 4th Fwd Spt Bn	6 June 03/31 Jan 04
Sergeant	Eliu Mier-Sandoval	KIA	Co A, 4th Fwd Spt Bn	31 January 2004
Specialist	Holly McGeogh	KIA	Co A, 4th Fwd Spt Bn	31 January 2004
Captain	Timothy J. Morrow	WIA	HHC	28 October 2003
Private	Ronald Bailey	WIA	HHC	1 January 2004
Specialist	Juan Cantu	WIA	HHC	23 July 2003
Specialist	Claude J. Goodwin, IV	WIA	HHC	2 August 2003
Specialist	Danny Harris	WIA	HHC	23 July 2003
Private	John A. Lyons	WIA	HHC	4 July 2003
Staff Sergeant	Felipe A. Madrid	WIA	HHC	16 December 2003
Specialist	Lovie V. Moran, Jr.	WIA	HHC	1 January 2004
Specialist	Percell E. Phillips, Jr.	WIA	HHC	17 July 2003
Specialist	Stewart G. Simmons	WIA	HHC	2 August 2003

Sergeant First Class	Charles E. Chenault	WIA	Co A	2 September 2003
Staff Sergeant	Brad T. Owens	WIA	Co A	23 July 2003
Second Lieutenant	Warren S. Litherland	WIA	Co B	16 December 2003
Private First Class	Joel S. Deguzman	WIA	Co B	4 June 2003
Sergeant	Gary L. Dowd	WIA	Co B	16 December 2003
Private First Class	Stephen R. Fink	WIA	Co B	4 July 2003
Specialist	Leonard T. Johnson	WIA	Co B	12 October 3003
Staff Sergeant	John A. Lewis	WIA	Co B	4 July 2003
Private First Class	Timothy M. Moore	WIA	Co B	4 June 2003
Sergeant	Charles A. Myers	WIA (x2)	Co B	4 June & 4 July 2003
Specialist	Devon E. Pierce	WIA	Co B	4 June 2003
Private	Joshua M. Schoellman	WIA	Co B	5 June 2003
Sergeant First Class	Joseph T. Walden	WIA	Co B	4 July 2003
Sergeant First Class	David M. White	WIA	Co B	4 June 2003
Private First Class	Joshua L. Whitson	WIA	Co B	4 July 2003
Specialist	Ronald E. Woods, Jr.	WIA	Co B	4 July 2003
Private Second Class	Jorge M. Zamora, Jr.	WIA	Co B	4 June 2003
Captain	Bradley L. Boyd	WIA	Co C	16 December 2003
Specialist	Bradley Burns	WIA	Co C	19 January 2003
Private First Class	Sergio Cardenas	WIA	Co C	25 April 2003
Staff Sergeant	Roger Garcia	WIA	Co C	25 April 2003
Specialist	William Gilstrap	WIA	Co C	4 January 2004
Staff Sergeant	Matthew K. Leasau	WIA	Co C	6 June 2003
Sergeant First Class	James D. Parker	WIA	Co C	25 April 2003
Specialist	Edward M. Stephenson	WIA	Co C	1 October 2003
Private First Class	Rodrigo Vargas	WIA	Co C	16 December 2003
Corporal	William A. Velez	WIA	Co C	25 April 2003
Private	Antonio Hernandez	WIA	Co C, 3-66 Armor	20 October 2003
Second Lieutenant	Ali Adnan	WIA	Co A, 4th Fwd Spt Bn	2 September 2003

Captain	Curt Kuetemeyer	WIA	Co A, 4th Fwd Spt Bn	1 October 2003
Specialist	Aldolfo Lopez	WIA	Co A, 4th Fwd Spt Bn	1 October 2003
Private First Class	William G. McBroom	WIA	Co A, 4th Fwd Spt Bn	2 September 2003
Staff Sergeant	Darrell W. Patton	WIA	Co A, 4th Fwd Spt Bn	6 June 2003
Specialist	Michael L. Regehr	WIA	Co A, 4th Fwd Spt Bn	2 September 2003
Staff Sergeant	Charles P. Darrah, Jr.	WIA	362nd PSYOPS Det.	12 October 2003
Sergeant	Antonio R. Carrizales	WIA	362nd PSYOPS Det.	12 October 2003
Specialist	Malcolm X. Mosely	WIA	362nd PSYOPS Det.	12 October 2003

GLOSSARY

KIA — Killed in Action
WIA — Wounded in Action

"I'LL THINK OF YOU"
By Steve Russell

I wait for your face
To return from a distant place.
I seek your words,
Mental speeches that are never heard.

Refrain:

And today I thought of you,
Of the full life that you never knew;
Of the world that passed you by;
Of your loved ones, you never told "Goodbye."
So today, I'll think of you.

Free souls, steep price,
Proud flags, draped in sacrifice
Of youth, now gone
But the memories carry on.

Refrain:

And today I thought of you,
Of the full life that you never knew;
Of the world that passed you by;
Of your loved ones, you never told "Goodbye."
So today, I'll think of you.

SILENT STREAMS

Soft tan silhouette in the morning light.
Unknown heartache awaits sleeping hearts
half a world away.

Punctured metal, scratched and stained
with crimson streaks,
speaks to the violence of short hours before.

A struggle for life, his own and others.
Crimson smears pool on the floor,
covering the debris of life.

Half consumed,
deep crimson soaks into debris.

Riddled window, black dusted shield.
Fragments find homes in glass, metal, rubber.
Casings and links litter the floor, covered in crimson...

Jesse Halling lives no more,
His courage evident in
Silent Streams.

Written 7 June 2003 in Tikrit, Iraq hours after an attack on our Civil-Military Information & Coordination office (CMIC), as I inspected the vehicle from which Jesse Halling so bravely fought.

APPENDIX C
80TH INFANTRY DIVISION RECORDS

FOXTROT COMPANY, 2D BN, 319TH INFANTRY REGIMENT
Morning Report[34]
Glauchau, Germany April 1945
[Liberated Magdalena Rauhut (Winkel)]

---

34. 80th Division Digital Archives Project Morning Reports, http://www.80thdivision. com/WebArchives/MorningReports.html and http://www.80thdivision.com/ MorningReports/APR45/MR319F_APR45.pdf, accessed 21 March 2018. Very special thanks to the 80th Division Veterans Association: National Commander Paul Stutts, Senior Vice Commander Brian Faulconer, WWII Historian Andy Adkins, and National Chaplain Doug Knorr. Their dedication and very helpful web page (http:// www.80thdivision.com) greatly enabled my research.

FROM "HEADQUARTERS 319ᵀᴴ INFANTRY, OFFICE OF THE REGIMENTAL COMMANDER, APO 80, U.S. ARMY

Unit History (For Month of April), Section VII: Battles"[35]
[Liberated Magdalena Rauhut (Winkel)]

REPRODUCED AT THE NATIONAL ARCHIVES

SECTION VII - Battles (cont).

1. 15 April 1945. Glauchau, Germany.
2. Narrative account of action:
   a. Enemy action:
      The enemy in Glauchau chose to fight for every inch of
the city. They were armed with rifles, automatic weapons and bazookas.
One particularly strong point surrendered 60 officers and 200 men after
we issued them an ultimatum over a loudspeaker. The city was not officially reported cleared until the close of the period. Crimmitchau
was not as stubbornly defended. It was also cleared by the end of the
period. Meerane was occupied by our troops. 738 prisoners were gathered from these three cities; the majority of them coming from Glauchau.
Many officers were reported taken.
   b. Friendly action:
      No change in attachments. 3rd Bn CP located in Meerane.
No change in mission. 1st Bn pounded Crimmitschau with artillery during the early hours of the morning starting fires in several places.
At 0740 2nd Bn moved out to clear Glauchau. At 0810 3rd Bn closed in
Meerane and proceede d to clear the town meeting no opposition. Both
1st and 2nd Bn experienced considerable small arms fire and bazooka
fire in clearing their towns. Civilians engaged in extensive sniper
fire against our troops. 2nd Bn ran into a strong defensive position
in the center of Glauchau and knocked it out only after considerable
difficulty. TDs and Tks were fired at buildings at point blank range
to knock out enemy strongpoints. By 1220 1st Bn had moved through
their town but occasional sniping was still evident. Received Div FO
#37 giving 319th Inf the mission of relieving the 4th Armd Div when
they established bridgehead west of Chemnitz. 1st Bn 317th began relief of 1st Bn 319th at 1915. 2nd Bn cleared Glauchau at 2400. The
weapons used during the day's action consisted of rockets, 105mm WP,
grenades and bazookas.

35. 80th Division Digital Archives Project, http://www.80thdivision.com/
UnitHistories/319thInfReg_UnitHistory_APR45-partial_1.pdf accessed 21 March
2018.

80ᵀᴴ INFANTRY DIVISION RECORDS

Interview of the 80ᵗʰ Infantry Division Assistant Division Commander and Regimental Commanding Officer of the 319ᵗʰ Infantry Regiment[36]

[Liberated Magdalena Rauhut (Winkel)]

"The 2d Bn [319ᵗʰ Infantry Regiment] in the meantime moved at 1430 hours and detrucked behind the forward elements of the armor which were attacking GLACHAU (K3858). The 2d Bn went into an assembly area NW of the town [Gesau] in the group of buildings located at (K3659) and plans were worked out with the CO of the 51ˢᵗ Armd Inf Bn for the 2d Bn to take over at dawn and clear the town 15 April.

The 3d Bn remained in GERA for the evening as the promised relief did not appear until 141800 hours. Col COSTELLO decided that it was too late to move them up that night and ordered the 3d to move forward in the morning 15 April.

Col COSTELLO planned to move the 3d forward at dawn and clear MEERANE 9K3360) while the 1ˢᵗ cleaned out CRIMMITSHAU and the 2d Bn passed through the 51ˢᵗ Armd Inf Bn and wiped up the resistance in GLACHAU. MEERANE capitulated at 0800 hours 15 April as the 3d enveloped it from the S and W. The 1ˢᵗ Bn had little difficulty routing out snipers from the southern half of CRIMMITSCHAU as the bulk of the defenders had fled during the night.

In GLACHAU liaison had been maintained with the 51ˢᵗ Armd Inf Bn throughout the night. The town was about 75% cleared out but the narrow streets prohibited the use of tanks

---

36. 80th Division Digital Archives Project, pp 10 – 12, http://www.80thdivision.com/AfterActionReports/319th_DriveFromGothatoChemnitz_08-18APR45.pdf accessed 21 March 2018.

and TDs. The enemy Inf was anchored in the buildings and was stoutly resisting any further penetration with bazooka and MG fire. Resistance seemed to be centered around a barracks in the eastern edge of the town. The 51st had taken out approximately 2000 PWs the day before but when the 2 moved in at 0730 hours 15 April it became involved in a bitter house to house struggle necessitating a house to house search and seizure. About 200 SS troops were finally cornered in the barracks and fanatically resisted all efforts to dig them out. Five hundred seventy eight (578) PWs had been taken by 2000 hours. A medical jeep carrying a wounded German soldier and two German nurses plus one American medic went by the barracks; a bazooka shot killed them all. The assault elements of the 2d Bn thereupon closed in on the barracks. When the barracks and the last resistance in GLACHAU had been taken at 2330 hours there were still only 578 PWs.

The Bns remained in position during the night while the armor of CCA and the Cav Sqdn moved around to the E of GLAUCHAU prepared to strike at CHEMNITZ."[37]

---

37. 80th Division Digital Archives Project, pp 10 – 12, http://www.80thdivision.com/ AfterActionReports/319th_DriveFromGothatoChemnitz_08-18APR45.pdf accessed 21 March 2018.

APPENDIX D

319TH INFANTRY
80TH INFANTRY DIVISION
VETERANS

BURT R. MARSH
&
CHARLES O. FAULCONER, SR.

Burt R. Marsh
Company M, 3d Battalion

Born 4-3-1926 in Seneca Falls, NY, graduate of Menderes Academy on 6-27-1944. As I reached my 18th birthday 4-3-1944, I received a letter from our local draft board ordering me to report to the local draft board on 6-6-1944 to have a physical examination in Rochester, NY to determine my draft status. Passing my physical, classified A-1 into the U.S. Army. I graduated 6-27-1944, received my "Greetings" from U.S. War Department requesting me to report to the draft board 8-9-1944 for induction in the U.S. Army at Rochester, NY.

Arriving at Fort Dix, NJ on 8-10-1944 for my introduction to the U.S. Army, more physicals, several orientations, explaining the rules and operations of the army. On 8-20-1944 I was placed on a troop train, destination unknown, for 16 week infantry training for preparation to serve with an army unit at war. Arriving at camp Blanding, FL on 8-23-1944, I was welcomed to the camp by the Commanding Officer, I received my uniform (fatigues) rifle and shown my sleeping quarters, a 12 man wooden structure. The training was touch, the sergeants and instructions were tough and after 16 weeks of tough training, I graduated as a tough infantry soldier. The training was the learning to use all infantry weapons, my specialty was training on heavy weapons, the 30 caliber water-cooled heavy machine gain and the 81 mil. mortar weapon. Basic training ended 12-18-1944. I returned to Ft. Dix and was issued a 10 day (delay in route) furlough with orders to report to Ft. Meade, NY at 1-1-1945. I went home with family for 10 days. At Ft. Meade, I went through more physicals, more shots, etc., preparing me for overseas duty in Europe.

Left Ft. Meade, 1-8-1945 for New York City to board the Queen Elizabeth for our trip to Europe. Leaving NYC on 1-10-1945 with 21,000 troops aboard. Arriving at Liverpool, England 1-14-1945, boarded a troop train for a trip across England to South Hampton, boarded a British ship for the trip across the English Channel arriving in Lahavre France, boarded a French troop train for trip across France arriving in Luxembourg City 1-18-1945. Boarded 2-1/2 ton truck for a trip to a small village, Nocher, Luxembourg, to be assigned to Co. M. 319 Inf. Reg., of the 80th Division as a 30 caliber water cooled heavy machine gunner, 1st squad, 1st platoon. There was a foot of snow on the ground, temperature in the 20's we were in battle the next 5 days, liberations several villages, resistance was light except for some artillery fire the German troops had retreated to their home land and the Siegfried Line (West wall) to set their defense in preparation for our invasion to their home land. On 1-29-1945 the 80th Division was pulled off the front lines for a 6 day (R and R), rest and restoration. We boarded 2-1/2 ton trucks and transported to small village outside of Luxembourg City and placed in private homes. 4 troops to a house, I was in the village of Steinsel meeting the Thoma Family. I made friends with the family twin daughters.

On 2-6-1945, we left Steinsel by truck and back to the front lines and ready to invade Germany and their West Wall (Siegfried Line) But first we had to cross the flooded "Our River".

The 150th Engineering Battalion was trying to build a foot bridge across the Our River, the river was so swift and receiving heavy artillery fire, the bridge wasn't completed until the night of 2-11-1945.

The first and second battalions crossed in assaults boats on 2-7, 8, 9, 10, 1945. Receiving many causalities, due to heavy artillery fire and strong resistance on the German side of the river. Each night the Third Battalion went to the river to cross, but no assault boats were available, (lost many boats due to the swift current) and heavy artillery fire, we were forced to pull back. The night of 2-11-1945, the Engineers completed part of the foot bridge allowing the Third Battalion to cross, however, we had to wade the last thirty yards in knee deep water.

The following night 2-12-1945 we attack the Siegfried Line taking or capturing many pill boxes under heavy artillery fire all night long. The night was pitch black, raining, temperatures near freezing, but we kept moving forward. At daybreak, we ended the attack only to come under mortar fire from a pill box about a quarter mile in front of us. Since we had heavy casualties during the night, we set up a defense line for three days, we attack the pill box that was firing mortars on us on 2-16-1945, only to retreat because of heavy mortar fire and we were undermanned, we never did capture that pill box. Our first gunner was killed during this attack. Another company worked their way around us and captured it, taking 47 prisoners.

On 2-19-1945 the 319th assembled at Wallendorf, Germany to regroup, reorganized, and resupply and receive new replacements.

On 2-20-1945 we went on attack in a Northwest direction toward Bitburg, taking many villages with the fighting very heavy. We reached Bitburg on 3-7-1945.

On 3-9-1945 the 80th Division moved South 40 miles by truck to Merckel, Germany to relieve the 76th Division. On 3-10-1945 we went on attack in an Eastern direction toward Kaiserslautern, Germany, passing through the Siegfried Line again, capturing many village and reaching Kaiserslautern 3-21-1945.

On 3-22-1945, we attack in a Northern directions toward Worms, Germany and then on to Pfeddersheim, Germany on 3-25-1945 to cross the Rhine River, The fighting was spotty, taken many prisoners.

On 3-27-1945, we crossed the Rhine River on a moon light night in assault boats under light artillery fire, little resistance as we landed, continuing on to cross the main river on 3-28-1945 in assault boats, meeting little resistance.

We continued our attack in a Northly direction to Kassel, Germany arriving 4-3-1945 (my 19th Birthday) fighting was very heavy in and around Kassel, by 4-6-1945 the city was declared clear.

On 4-7-1945, we attack in an Eastern direction liberating villages of Gotha, Erfurt, Weimar, Buchenwald, Jena, Gera, Glauchau, Meerane just shy of Chemnitz on 4-16-1945. The resistance was light and spotty in these villages. I do remember passing by Buchenwald concentration camp and seeing its prisoners in their striped prison garb. Since we were on attack, we did not stop, I had no idea of what I saw was a death camp.

On 4-17-1945, the 80th Division was loaded on trucks for an assignment in Austria traveling through Bamberg, Nuremberg, Regensburg arriving in Giessenbach, Austria on 5-1-1945. We met no resistance while in Austria through 5-8-1945. We took a few prisoners on our way to Steyr, Austria. That's where the 319th ended its fighting.

Since I wasn't eligible to return to USA, I spent 13 months of duty as part of the occupation of Germany. When the 80th Division returned to USA in November 1945, I transferred to 102nd Division, when they went to USA in Feb. 1946. I transferred to the Big Red, 1st Division located in Regensburg, Germany. I really did not have any specific duties because I played baseball in the summer and basketball in the winter.

I received my going home orders 6-6-1946, arrived at La-Harvre, France 6-10-1946, boarded a US Liberty ship, the US West Minster, arriving in New York City 6-20-1946. A train to Fort Dix, NJ and received my honorable discharge 6-27-1946. Thus, ending my army life.

On 11-1-1952 I married Barbara (Stahl) and have two daughters, Tammi and Tina and two granddaughters, Heather and Lindsay. Employed for 37 years with New York State Electric and Gas Corp. retiring in 1991 as a Customer Service Manager. Currently living in Columbus OH with my daughter Tina and her husband Jeff.

Burt R. Marsh
10-25-2018

Charles Olan Faulconer Sr.[38]
Company A, 1st Battalion
March 22, 1926 — December 2, 2018

"Charles Olan Faulconer, Sr. of Monroe, Virginia died December 2, 2018
in Florida.

Charles was born March 22,1926 in Monroe to his parents
Charles Andrew Faulconer and Myrtle Inez Floyd Faulconer.
Charles was preceded in death by his wife Louise McCord Faulconer, to whom he was married for sixty-five years, having married June 15, 1951.

Together they embraced their hometown of Monroe and
Amherst County, raising their sons and contributing to their
community, where Charles served as postmaster at the Monroe
Post Office 1951-1977. A decorated veteran of WWII, Charles
was a member of Patton's 3rd Army, 80th division, 319th Infantry Company A. He was wounded at age 18 on February 8, 1945,

---

38. Obituary of Charles Olan Faulconer, Sr., Dignity Memorial, https://www.
dignitymemorial.com/obituaries/madison-heights-va/charles-faulconer-8077754
(accessed 22 March 2019)

fighting from a forward position on the front lines in Germany, during the Battle of the Bulge, the last major German offensive on the Western Front during the war. For his actions, Charles was awarded the Bronze Star, the Purple Heart, and, just two years ago, the French Legion of Honour, the highest decoration awarded in France.

Maintaining his dedication to his home and family in Virginia during retirement, Charles also became determined to understand the context of his military service, and he traveled back to Europe to find the battlefield of his youth. On his first visit, he was surprised, honored, and humbled to be awarded a medal of appreciation from the Grand Duchy of Luxembourg.

Inspired by the continuing gratitude of the citizens of Luxembourg and France for the service of all Allied troops, Charles returned to Europe a few years later in 2011, with his wife, sons, daughters-in-law, and grandchildren, where he was able to pinpoint the very foxhole he fought from in Luxembourg before being wounded the next day after crossing the Our River into Wallendorf, Germany. Charles was finally able to show and tell the fullness of his story to his family, a story emblematic of the sacrifices of The Greatest Generation, in which a young man from a small train town in Virginia traveled thousands of miles to help win a world war, a story similar to that of many of his comrades in arms.

Charles was active in the Battle of the Bulge Association and the 80th Division Veterans Association, attending reunions with his wife and sons. Charles grew up at a time when Monroe was a bustling village centered around a Southern Railway train yard. His first job was delivering newspapers for 25 cents a day. He later took grocery orders from Monroe residents, delivering groceries and food from the four stores and the restaurant that were in business in Monroe at the time.

He began attending Monroe School when it was built in 1935, and he graduated from Madison Heights High School. Though he lived his entire life as a Monroe resident, Charles' curiosity about the world led him to travel to 49 states in the United States (except Hawaii), most often traveling by RV with family. He was a member of the Blue Ridge Winnies camping club for 23 years and part of the Holiday Travel community in Leesburg, Florida. He often traveled with his children and his grandchildren. With family, he visited Germany, Luxembourg, Belgium, France, Ireland, England, and Scotland.

He was a member of First Baptist Church of Monroe, where he was baptized as a child. The landmarks and stories of Monroe lived in his memory. He had gifts with animals, growing vegetables, and mechanical things, and he also had a creative side, taking pictures, and preserving historic photos. He encouraged both his children and grandchildren to learn to play music, enjoy the outdoors, travel, and work hard.

Charles is survived by three sons and daughters-in-law and their families: Charles Faulconer, Jr. and Susan Faulconer of McCormick, SC; Robert "Rick" Faulconer and Jeanne Faulconer of Chesterfield, VA; and Brian Faulconer and Mary Faulconer of Holly Springs, NC. His grandchildren are Laura Faulconer Leslie, Emily Faulconer Purcell, Kevin McCord Faulconer, Patrick Faulconer, Nick Faulconer, Cameron Faulconer, and Jake Faulconer. His great-grandchildren are Page Jeromy Pell, Isla Louise Leslie, Ivy Monroe Leslie, and Samantha Purcell. He is also survived by his brother, Paul Faulconer and wife Audrey Faulconer of Madison Heights; he was predeceased by his siblings Lucy Leavitt Faulconer of Lane, Oregon; Faye Faulconer Clark Ford of South Boston; and Hayes Faulconer of Monroe.

A graveside service will be conducted 1:00 p.m., Friday, December 7, 2018, at Fort Hill Memorial Park with the Rev. Steve

Tyree officiating. Military Honors will be presented by the American Legion Post 36 from Altavista and Post 232 from Gretna.

The family will receive friends 5-7 p.m., Thursday, December 6, 2018, at Whitten Monelison Chapel.

Charles Faulconer was a true American Hero and a member of our Greatest Generation. He will be remembered for his energy, integrity, and indomitable spirit, embodied in the slogan of the 80th Infantry: "Only Moves Forward.""[39]

---

39. Obituary of Charles Olan Faulconer, Sr., Dignity Memorial, https://www.dignitymemorial.com/obituaries/madison-heights-va/charles-faulconer-8077754 (accessed 22 March 2019)

APPENDIX E

83ᴿᴰ INFANTRY DIVISION RECORDS

Headquarters 83D Infantry Division, APO 83, U.S. Army,
16 May 1945

329ᵗʰ Infantry
"Section I, After Action Report, April 1945"[40]
[Liberated Horst Rauhut]

11 APRIL 1945

"Another day of rapid progress followed. The 1ˢᵗ drove into the
town of BAD HARZBURG, while the 2ⁿᵈ moved by to the
north and spearheaded against light resistance. Here and there,
as at LANGELN, (D1072), determined resistance was encountered. Near DERENBERG (D1868) a column of approximately
700 British and American PW's was liberated. The 3ʳᵈ Bn, once
started, was hard to stop. They drove east from VIENEBERG,
clearing one town after another. Though their zone ran to the
north of HALBERSTADT (D2671) the 3ʳᵈ Bn, finding themselves closest to the city, drove into the city against heavy small

40. 83rd Infantry Division Documents; 329th Infantry Regiment pp 4-5:
https://83rdinfdivdocs.org/units/329th-ir/ , After Action Reports April 1945
https://83rdinfdivdocs.org/documents/329th/AAR/AAR_329_APR1945.pdf accessed
24 March 2018.

arms resistance. The 2nd Bn assisted to complete the capture of the city. Orders having been received to dash to the ELBE, the 3rd Bn did not stop in HALBERSTADT, but continued to push on to GRONINGEN (D3976) where the fight against stubborn opposition occurred. The 2nd halted for the night at WEGELEBEN (D3670), where somewhat lighter opposition was encountered. The 1st Bn mopped up what remained of resistance in HALBERSTADT. This day's work brought the regiment 46kms closer to the ELBE, resulted in the clearing of the large city of HALBERSTADT, the cities of BAD HARZBURG and DERENBURG, along with 31 other towns and villages, and the capture of 5428 PW's, approximately 4000 of whom were hospitalized."

LTC Granville A. Sharpe
Battalion Commander whose unit helped clear Halberstadt
2nd Battalion, 329 "Buckshot" Infantry Regiment[41]

---

41. Goguen, Raymond J., Sgt., 329 "Buckshot" Infantry Regiment : A History, 1945. USAHEC, Call Number 603-3291945 / 2

1st & 3rd Battalions, Commanders and Staffs[42]

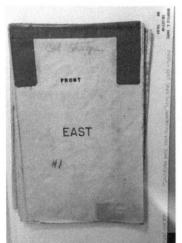

Map w/Halberstadt insert used by LTC Granville A. Sharpe in WWII
Battalion Commander
2nd Battalion, 329 "Buckshot" Infantry Regiment[43]

---

42. Ibid.

43. Granville A. Sharpe Collection, Series IV Maps, circa 1945-circa 1950, Box 7 of 8, US Army Heritage & Education Center.

APPENDIX F

Magdalena Rauhut Christmas letters written during WWII when Mom was 11 years old.

Magdalena Rauhut Letter 1 (KLV Lager to Glauchau) 22 Dec 1942

December 22, 1942

Dear ones in Glauchau,

I thought you should have a letter for Christmas so I wrote this letter. I wish you a happy and blessed feast…[unreadable]… didn't get the package…? I thought I had for everyone something, not just for Uncle Ernst. It does not look like Christmas here. The sun is shining. I am feeling very good. I am healthy and excited. Now we have two more days to sleep and then is Christmas Eve. We play a Christmas song [or play?] that is named "Christmas in Sweigenreich" ["Christmas with the Dwarfs"]. I am a little difficult [unreadable]. Now I have to close. Many loving greetings for Christmas and a happy and loving Christmas.

Your Lanchen

Days later, Mom sent another letter:

December 30, 1942

"Dear Uncle Ernst!

Greetings to your 50th Birthday. I hope you can celebrate your birthday. I often think back on the good times with you. Now I have to tell you about Christmas. First, thank you for the loving Christmas package which I got this morning at 06:30am. The bell sounded and we stormed into the day room, but here has to be more quiet. We were surprised the Christmas Tree was nicely decorated. It had apples and golden?, small stars decorated and golden? tree combs were also found on them.

After we sang some songs and said poems, we played a Christmas story called "Christmas Time with the Dwarfs." I was also a little dwarf. After the play we got our packages. Even the camp thought about us. We got a book entitled, "Hitler Abseits vom Alltag"[44] ["Hitler Away from Everyday Life"]. Then we got a group photograph [unreadable] stand for the picture. Saucer full of sweets. We delighted in it. Also a photo album with picture book was found in the things from camp. From home I got a big package whereon Tante Grete had a Pupen [pillow] and also other things you could find in the package, sweets also. Even Gerhardt did not forget me!

This is enough.

Greetings again. Your Lanchen

---

44. Piece of Nazi propaganda published in 1937 which includes 100 "cameo" pictures of Hitler. "100 Bilddokumente aus der Umgebung des Fuhrers". Given the nature of the KLV program, it is not surprising that the secularization of Christmas included such a "gift" and all the more striking that Mom's request to sing Christian Christmas songs was positively received by her leader. See SILENT NIGHT (Christmas Reflections) for more.

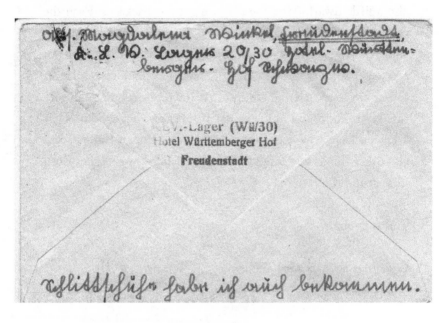

Magdalena Rauhut Letter Env B (KLV to Glauchau) 30 Dec 1942

Stamp: Kinderlandverschickung (KLV).-Lager (Wh/30), Hotel Württenberger Hof, Freudenstadt, Germany German program[45] At bottom: "I also got some snow shoes"

---

45. Kinderlandverschickung (KLV) ["send children to the country"]. See Nicholos Stargardt's, "The German War, A Nation Under Arms, 1939-1945", pp114-117; 398-399, for a good description of the Nazi's children evacuation program. The KLV became both a means to secure the children's safety as well as an indoctrination opportunity for the Nazis.

ABOUT THE AUTHORS

29 May 2011
Michael Winfred and Horst Wilfried Rauhut
("He who makes" and "He who wants" Peace)

1985 to 2019
Colonel Mike Rauhut
Infantry, U.S. Army

Mike Rauhut is the son and brother of German immigrants; Horst and Magdalena Rauhut, and sisters Monika and Birgit. Born to immigrants in Washington, D.C., Mike was drawn to serve and recently concluded 34 years of U.S. Army service. Early in his service, Mike met his beautiful and talented wife Sandy, also a child of German immigrants, and together have two children: Hannah and Jacob.

Growing up in Hinsdale, New York, Mike graduated from the United States Military Academy at West Point in 1989 and commissioned in the Infantry. He commanded at the platoon-, company-, battalion-, and brigade-levels. Mike also served in various staff, faculty, and leadership positions culminating most recently as the Assistant Chief of Staff for the International Security Assistance Force in Kabul; a Military Fellow at the Council on Foreign Relations in New York City; the ambassadorial military adviser to the US Mission to the United Nations; and the Director of the U.S. Army Peacekeeping and Stability Operations Institute. His assignments have taken him to locales as varied as Georgia & Germany, Saudi Arabia & South Sudan, Iraq, Korea, and Afghanistan. Mike holds a Master of Science in Operations Research and a Master of Strategic Studies.

CPSIA information can be obtained
at www.ICGtesting.com
Printed in the USA
BVHW081747291119
564966BV00002B/8/P